BOOK OF WORLD RECORDS

BY
BLYTHE BOUZA
MICHAEL BRIGHT
CHRIS HAWKES
ABIGAIL MITCHELL
CYNTHIA O'BRIEN
MIKE ROBBINS
DONALD SOMMERVILLE
ANTONIA VAN DER MEER

Copyright © 2025 by Scholastic Inc.

All rights reserved. Published by Scholastic Inc., *Publishers since 1920*.
SCHOLASTIC and associated logos are trademarks and/or registered
trademarks of Scholastic Inc.

Due to this book's publication date, the majority of statistics are current as
of February 2025. The publisher does not have any control over and does not
assume any responsibility for author or third-party websites or their content.

No part of this publication may be reproduced, stored in a retrieval system,
or transmitted in any form or by any means, electronic, mechanical,
photocopying, recording, or otherwise, or used to train any artificial
intelligence technologies, without written permission of the publisher.
For information regarding permission, write to Scholastic Inc., Attention:
Permissions Department, 557 Broadway, New York, NY 10012.

This book was created and produced by Toucan Books Limited.

Designer: Lee Riches
Editors: Anna Southgate, Rachel Malig
Proofreader: Marilyn Knowlton
Index: Vanessa Bird
Toucan would like to thank Cian O'Day for picture research.

ISBN 978-1-5461-8240-5

10 9 8 7 6 5 4 3 2 1   25 26 27 28 29

Printed in the U.S.A.   40

First printing, 2025

CONTENTS

4

CHAPTER 1
MUSIC MAKERS

22

CHAPTER 2
STAGE & SCREEN

44

CHAPTER 3
ON THE MOVE

60

CHAPTER 4
SUPER STRUCTURES

82

CHAPTER 5
HIGH TECH

108

CHAPTER 6
AMAZING ANIMALS

154

CHAPTER 7
INCREDIBLE EARTH

180

CHAPTER 8
STATE STATS

234

CHAPTER 9
SPORTS STARS

278 Index
286 Photo Credits

CHAPTER 1
MUSIC MAKERS

END OF THE ERAS
LAST SHOW OF SWIFT'S TOUR

After 149 shows on five different continents, Taylor Swift finally completed the Eras Tour in Vancouver in December 2024. It is believed to have been watched live by 10.1 million fans in jam-packed arenas around the globe. The tour broke records when it became the first to earn more than $1 billion, but by the final performance, it reportedly brought in an amazing $2,077,618,725, plus $400 million in merchandise sales.

SONG OF THE SUMMER
"ESPRESSO" GOES VIRAL

The summer of 2024 was the summer of Sabrina Carpenter, with everybody singing along to "Espresso"—the first single from her 2024 album *Short n' Sweet*. Catchy lyrics and a disco beat, as well as Sabrina's trademark humor, made it undeniably popular, and *Billboard* named it the no. 1 global song of the summer. Both the single and the album earned Carpenter Grammy Awards in 2025 (Best Pop Solo Performance and Best Pop Vocal Album).

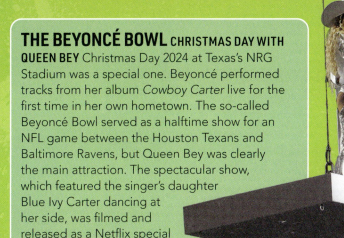

THE BEYONCÉ BOWL CHRISTMAS DAY WITH

QUEEN BEY Christmas Day 2024 at Texas's NRG Stadium was a special one. Beyoncé performed tracks from her album *Cowboy Carter* live for the first time in her own hometown. The so-called Beyoncé Bowl served as a halftime show for an NFL game between the Houston Texans and Baltimore Ravens, but Queen Bey was clearly the main attraction. The spectacular show, which featured the singer's daughter Blue Ivy Carter dancing at her side, was filmed and released as a Netflix special on December 27.

K-POP QUEEN FIRST SOLOIST TO

WIN BEST K-POP ARTIST Lisa made history in 2024 as the first soloist ever to win the top K-pop Award at the VMAs—a title previously held by BTS and Lisa's own girl group, BLACKPINK. It was a big year for the singer and rapper, who formed her own record label (Lloud) and had her first *Billboard* no. 1 hit with her song "Rockstar." According to Lloud, "Rockstar" got more than 100 million views in just two weeks, making it a huge success.

A BOLD NEW STAR CHAPPELL SPEAKS

OUT Chappell Roan won Best New Artist at the 2024 VMAs and delivered a fiery midshow performance. Yet she made the news for a very different reason that night when videos showed her clapping back at a photographer who shouted at her on the red carpet. Roan became an overnight superstar in 2024, and she spoke openly on social media about the pressures of being in the spotlight. The artist went on to win Best New Artist at the Grammys in February 2025.

"BIRDS OF A FEATHER"
BILLIE EILISH

MOST-STREAMED SONGS OF 2024

Billie Eilish / "Birds of a Feather"
1,807,862,651

Sabrina Carpenter / "Espresso"
1,794,993,262

Benson Boone / "Beautiful Things"
1,722,910,524

Lady Gaga / "Die with a Smile"
1,458,746,731

FloyyMenor / "Gata Only"
1,374,434,294

Artist / song

200,000   1,000,000   2,000,000

Number of streams

With more than 1.8 billion plays, "Birds of a Feather" by Billie Eilish was the most-streamed song on Spotify in 2024. Released in July, the song debuted at no. 13 on the *Billboard* Hot 100 chart, reaching a peak of no. 5 in its thirteenth week. The release of the song's music video in September brought it to the no. 2 spot on the Hot 100—Eilish's highest placement since her 2020 song "Therefore I Am." Given the song's popularity on Spotify, it comes as no surprise to learn that "Birds of a Feather" was nominated for Record of the Year, Song of the Year, and Best Solo Pop Performance at the 2025 Grammy Awards.

THE TORTURED POETS DEPARTMENT
TAYLOR SWIFT

The Tortured Poets Department was the most-streamed album on Spotify in 2024. Released in April, Taylor Swift's newest album broke plenty of records, with first album to top 300 million streams in one day among them. It was also the first album to have more than one billion streams in the first week of its release. Self-described as a "lifeline" album, *Tortured Poets* features several songs that hint at the artist's rocky romantic past. To commemorate Swift's "most-streamed" status on the platform, Spotify added a Wrapped badge to her artist profile. This marks the start of a feature that the company declares will be an annual distinction for future artists achieving the same feat.

Most-liked video on YouTube
"DESPACITO"

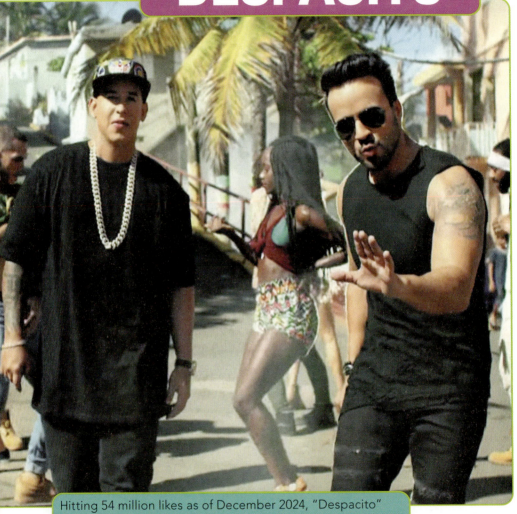

Hitting 54 million likes as of December 2024, "Despacito" remains the most-liked video on YouTube. The Puerto Rican dance track by Luis Fonsi, which features Daddy Yankee and Justin Bieber, came out in 2017, and within six months it became the most-streamed song in history. It's no surprise that it also became the first music video to notch up five, six, seven, and eight billion views on YouTube. That's not to say it's everybody's favorite. According to YouTube's stats, the video is also in the top 20 most-disliked videos on the platform, with more than five million dislikes before YouTube made them invisible.

TAYLOR SWIFT

Star musician Taylor Swift continues to break records as she becomes the only living artist to simultaneously have ten albums on the *Billboard* 200 chart. Swift achieved this in both March and May of 2024, with her albums ranking as follows in May: *Folklore: The Long Pond Studio Sessions* (no. 3), *Midnights* (no. 4), *Lover* (no. 10), *Folklore* (no. 12), *1989* (no. 21), *Reputation* (no. 22), *Red (Taylor's Version)* (no. 27), *evermore* (no. 29), *Fearless (Taylor's Version)* (no. 41), and *Speak Now* (no. 66). Four other artists—the Beatles, David Bowie, Whitney Houston, and Prince—have achieved a similar feat, but only after their deaths (or, in the case of the Beatles, after the deaths of John Lennon and George Harrison).

First rapper to top *Billboard* Hot 100 chart

DRAKE

Drake released his album *If You're Reading This It's Too Late* through iTunes on February 12, 2015. The digital album sold 495,000 units in its first week and entered the *Billboard* 200 at no. 1, making Drake the first rap artist ever to top the chart. The album also helped Drake secure another record: most hits on the *Billboard* Hot 100 at one time. On March 7, 2015, Drake had fourteen hit songs on the chart, matching the record the Beatles have held since 1964. Since releasing his first hit single, "Best I Ever Had," in 2009, Drake has seen many of his singles go multiplatinum, including "Hotline Bling," which had eighteen weeks at no. 1 on the *Billboard* Hot 100.

FUERZA REGIDA

The 2024 *Billboard* Music Award for Top Duo/Group went to Fuerza Regida. This is the second year running that the group has won this award, proof that Mexican music continues to have a strong following in the United States. The band made waves in 2023 with their song "Bebe Dame," a collaboration with Grupo Frontera, and released tracks with Becky G, Shakira, and rapper Myke Towers. While 2023 marked their first win in this category, Fuerza Regida has been making music since 2015 and released their ninth studio album in 2024.

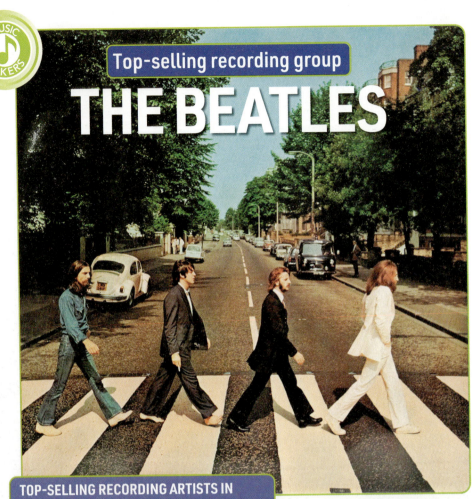

Top-selling recording group
THE BEATLES

TOP-SELLING RECORDING ARTISTS IN THE UNITED STATES
ALBUMS SOLD IN MILLIONS

Recording artist

	Millions
The Beatles	183
Garth Brooks	157
Elvis Presley	139
Eagles	120
Led Zeppelin	112.5

20 40 60 80 100 120 140 160 180 200
Millions

The Beatles continue to hold the record for best-selling recording group in the United States, with 183 million albums sold. The British band recorded their first album in September 1962 and made their *Billboard* debut with "I Want to Hold Your Hand." In 2023, the band broke another record, releasing a new single "Now and Then," which went straight to no. 1 on the UK charts—a record fifty-four years since their last no. 1 hit in that country.

Fastest K-pop star to hit one billion streams on Spotify

Jimin, singer in the K-pop boy band BTS, released his first solo EP, *FACE*, in March 2023. After only 393 days on the charts, Jimin's EP hit one billion streams on Spotify, making him the fastest K-pop artist ever to do so. Jimin's fellow bandmate, Jungkook, also has an EP that has hit one billion streams, but it took him sixteen days longer than Jimin to achieve this milestone. BTS is the most-streamed male group on Spotify, and Jimin's new record only makes the band more reputable.

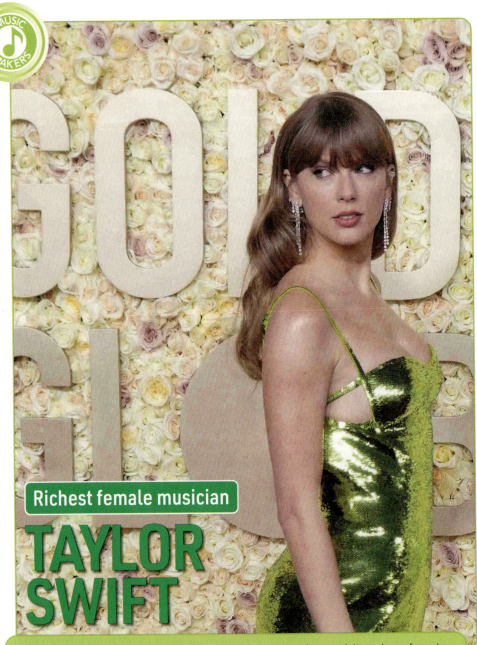

Richest female musician

TAYLOR SWIFT

In 2024, Taylor Swift officially dethroned Rihanna as the world's richest female musician, with a net worth of a whopping $1.6 billion. *Forbes* declared the illustrious Swift a billionaire in October 2023, most notably because of her earnings from her world-famous Eras Tour and widely streamed musical catalog. The thirty-four-year-old musician is also the first to become a billionaire based solely on her songs and performances, with her catalog alone racking up an impressive $600 million. Taylor Swift is the second-richest musician in the world, behind Jay-Z, who is worth an estimated $2.5 billion. With more music on the way, Swift may well come to take his crown!

"OLD TOWN ROAD"

From March through July 2019, rapper Lil Nas X's "Old Town Road" spent seventeen weeks in the no. 1 spot, pushing past "Despacito" from Luis Fonsi and Mariah Carey's "One Sweet Day," each of which spent sixteen weeks at the top of the charts. Lil Nas X's real name is Montero Hill, and he is from Atlanta, Georgia. He recorded the song himself, and people first fell in love with the catchy tune on TikTok. "Old Town Road" made it to the country charts, but it was later dropped for not being considered a country song. Disagreements about its genre only fueled interest in the song, however, and it subsequently hit no. 1. The song was then remixed and rerecorded with country music star Billy Ray Cyrus, whose wife at the time, Tish, encouraged him to become involved.

Musician with the most country music awards in one night

LAINEY WILSON

Lainey Wilson made country music history in November 2023, when she won five awards at the Country Music Awards. The triumph marked the most awards ever won by a female artist in a single night. The awards were Entertainer of the Year, Female Vocalist of the Year, Album of the Year (for *Bell Bottom Country*), Musical Event of the Year (for her collaboration with HARDY on "wait in the truck"), and Music Video of the Year ("wait in the truck"). Flames lit up the stage behind Wilson as she performed her hit "Wildflowers and Wild Horses" at the ceremony to cap off her big night.

BEYONCÉ

Musician with the most Grammys

Before 2024, Queen Bey was already reigning supreme as the musician with the most Grammys of all time with thirty-two awards to her name. Now she has thirty-five. At the 67th Grammy Awards, she won Album of the Year and Best Country Album for her 2024 release, *Cowboy Carter*, as well as Best Country Duo/Group Performance with Miley Cyrus ("Il Most Wanted"). After almost two decades of working in the music industry, this was Beyoncé's first Album of the Year win. She and her husband, Jay-Z, have ninety-seven Grammy nominations between them, making them the two most-nominated artists of all time.

First all-Spanish album to top the *Billboard* 200 chart

EL ÚLTIMO TOUR DEL MUNDO BAD BUNNY

Bad Bunny's album *El Último Tour del Mundo* (*The Last Tour in the World*) made music history in 2020, landing the top spot on *Billboard*'s 200 album chart. It's the first time in *Billboard*'s sixty-four-year history that an album performed entirely in Spanish has reached no. 1. The album, featuring a mix of Latin trap, reggaeton, and ska-punk, was one of three albums released by the Puerto Rican rapper, singer, and songwriter in 2020. His second album, *YHLQMDLG*, made it as high as no. 2 on the chart in March. Bad Bunny, whose birth name is Benito Antonio Martínez Ocasio, ended 2020 as Spotify's most-streamed artist of the year, amassing a staggering 8.3 billion streams.

TAYLOR SWIFT

The 2023 *Billboard* Music Awards (BBMAs) left Taylor Swift and Drake neck and neck as the BBMAs' most-awarded artists ever—each had an impressive total of thirty-nine awards. But that all changed dramatically at the 2024 BBMAs. Swift bagged ten awards—the most for any artist on the night—bringing her total to forty-nine Grammys in all, including awards for Top Artist, Top *Billboard* 200 Album, and Top Hot 100 Songwriter. Drake, meanwhile, won three awards—Top Rap Artist, Top Rap Male Artist, and Top Rap Album, taking his total to forty-two. Other prominent winners were country singers Zach Bryan and Morgan Wallen with five and four awards each.

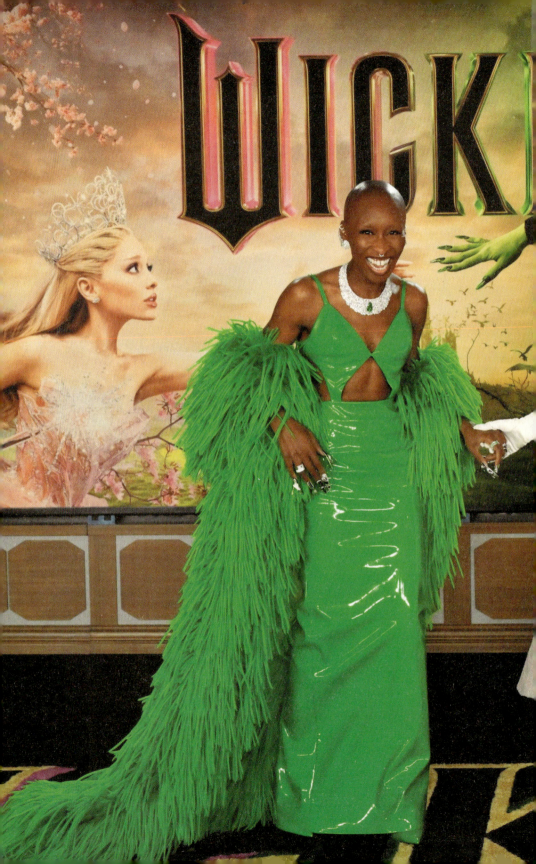

CHAPTER 2
STAGE & SCREEN

LIVING LIKE A MOVIE THE WES ANDERSON TREATMENT

TikTok went to film school in 2024 as users joined in the trend of filming moments of their everyday lives in the style of filmmaker Wes Anderson—known for his signature pastel aesthetic and quirky characters. The trend began when TikTok user Ava Williams posted a video of her family vacation mimicking the filmmaker's signature style. It got more than 12 million views, and soon others began to post their own versions.

PRECIOUS BOUNTY

THE MOST VALUABLE VINTAGE TOY IN THE WORLD

A *Star Wars* Boba Fett toy became the most valuable vintage toy ever when it sold for $525,000 in 2024. The 3.75-inch-tall action figure was made in 1979 and is famous for being able to fire missiles from its backpack. It's actually a prototype for a version that was made without a working rocket launcher due to safety concerns. This makes the prototype an incredibly rare and special collectors' item.

DREAM COLLABORATION
***SIMPSONS'* PREDICTION COMES TRUE**

A classic (1996!) episode of *The Simpsons* became reality in 2024 when Californian rappers Cypress Hill performed with the London Symphony Orchestra. The group performed at London's Royal Albert Hall in March with the full backing of the orchestra, calling it "a collaboration only *The Simpsons* could have predicted." In fact, the idea for the concert came from the 1996 episode, titled "Homerpalooza."

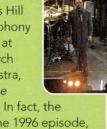

TIME TO PARTY! SPONGEBOB HITS A QUARTER-CENTURY MILESTONE

First making a splash in 1999, Nickelodeon's *SpongeBob SquarePants* celebrated twenty-five years in production in 2024. Entertaining many generations with the lovable sea sponge's underwater antics, infectious optimism, and adventures with pet snail Gary, the show has been translated into thirty languages and is watched by more than 400 million viewers worldwide each year.

HOLDING SPACE *WICKED* INTERVIEW GOES VIRAL

On the *Wicked* press tour, stars Cynthia Erivo and Ariana Grande talked about having a deep connection to their roles. In one interview, the host told Erivo that people were "holding space" for the lyrics to "Defying Gravity." Erivo's emotional response—and Grande's strange hold on one of her costar's manicured fingers—made holding space for "Defying Gravity" an instant meme.

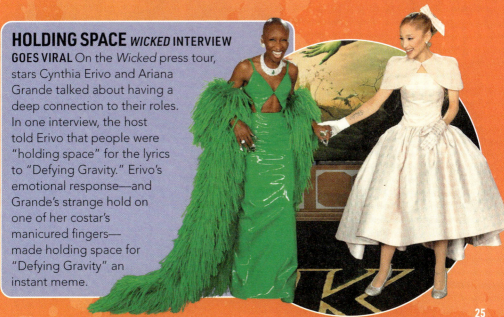

Longest-running scripted
TV show in the United States

THE SIMPSONS

The Simpsons entered its thirty-sixth season in 2024, continuing to break its own record as the longest-running American sitcom, cartoon, and scripted prime-time television show in history. The program will reach its 800th episode this season! The animated comedy, which first aired in December 1989, centers on the antics and everyday lives of the Simpson family. Famous guest stars with appearances in season thirty-six include John Cena, Tom Hanks, and Conan O'Brien. Fox has renewed the show for a thirty-seventh season, but the overall details are still pending.

Children's/family show with the most Emmys

HEARTSTOPPER

Taking five total awards at the 2022 Children's & Family Emmys, Netflix's *Heartstopper* is the winningest show in the ceremony's history so far. Based on a hugely successful graphic novel series of the same name, *Heartstopper* won awards for Outstanding Young Teen Series and for Outstanding Casting, while its creator, Alice Oseman, won for Outstanding Writing. The show's stars also did well: Kit Connor won Outstanding Lead Performance for his role as romantic lead Nick Nelson, while Olivia Colman won the award for Outstanding Guest Actor for playing his mom.

Most-watched television broadcast of 2024

SUPER BOWL LVIII

The 2023 Super Bowl, Super Bowl LVII, may have attracted nearly 115 million viewers, but the 2024 Super Bowl beat that record—an estimated 123.4 million people watched the game. Super Bowl LVIII saw the Kansas City Chiefs win yet again, this time against the San Francisco 49ers, with a final score of 25–22 in overtime. Besides watching for the game itself, viewers might have tuned in to see if singer Taylor Swift would be there to support her boyfriend, Chiefs player Travis Kelce, or for the famous halftime show, which featured Usher and a wide array of special guests.

INSIDE OUT 2

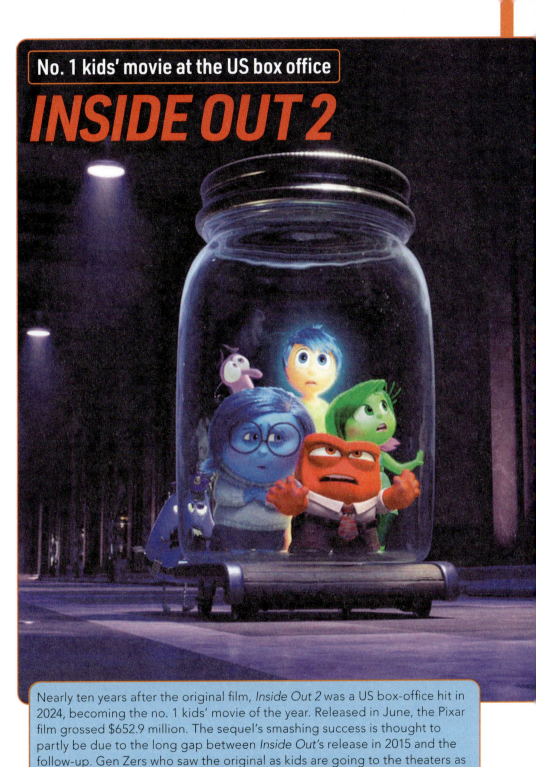

Nearly ten years after the original film, *Inside Out 2* was a US box-office hit in 2024, becoming the no. 1 kids' movie of the year. Released in June, the Pixar film grossed $652.9 million. The sequel's smashing success is thought to partly be due to the long gap between *Inside Out*'s release in 2015 and the follow-up. Gen Zers who saw the original as kids are going to the theaters as adults, looking to relive moments from their childhood. Now some of them even have kids of their own they can share *Inside Out 2* with!

Most popular kids' channel on YouTube
COCOMELON

The most popular kids' channel on YouTube is officially CoComelon, which specializes in vibrant and colorful 3D-animation videos of classic nursery rhymes and popular children's songs such as "Wheels on the Bus," "Baa Baa Black Sheep," "Humpty Dumpty," and more. CoComelon has 186 million subscribers and has generated a total of 192.4 billion views on its videos. As of May 2024, the famous channel is also the third-most-subscribed channel on the platform and the second-most viewed!

Most popular music channel on YouTube

T-SERIES

Music can change the world—or so says T-Series, the company that holds the spot as the most popular music channel on YouTube and the second-most-subscribed-to channel overall, right behind MrBeast. T-Series belongs to India's biggest music label. Currently, it has 280 million subscribers with over 20,000 videos uploaded. The channel's popularity is boosted by its ties to Bollywood—it often posts movie soundtracks and trailers, as well as Indi-pop music.

MOST POPULAR MUSIC CHANNELS ON YOUTUBE

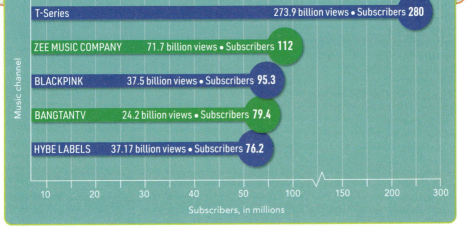

Music channel		
T-Series	273.9 billion views • Subscribers	**280**
ZEE MUSIC COMPANY	71.7 billion views • Subscribers	**112**
BLACKPINK	37.5 billion views • Subscribers	**95.3**
BANGTANTV	24.2 billion views • Subscribers	**79.4**
HYBE LABELS	37.17 billion views • Subscribers	**76.2**

10   20   30   40   50   100   150   200   300

Subscribers, in millions

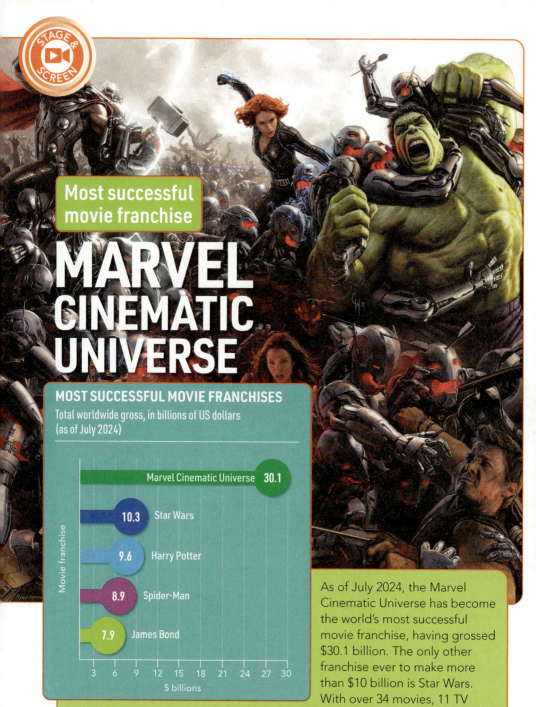

Most successful movie franchise

MARVEL CINEMATIC UNIVERSE

MOST SUCCESSFUL MOVIE FRANCHISES

Total worldwide gross, in billions of US dollars
(as of July 2024)

Movie franchise

Marvel Cinematic Universe	30.1
Star Wars	10.3
Harry Potter	9.6
Spider-Man	8.9
James Bond	7.9

$ billions
3   6   9   12   15   18   21   24   27   30

As of July 2024, the Marvel Cinematic Universe has become the world's most successful movie franchise, having grossed $30.1 billion. The only other franchise ever to make more than $10 billion is Star Wars. With over 34 movies, 11 TV series, and two specials, it's no mystery that the MCU is so hugely popular. Marvel's only release of 2024—*Deadpool & Wolverine*—was the top-grossing movie of the year. And the end of the MCU is nowhere in sight—Disney has three more films slated to come out in 2025, and has announced projects all the way into 2027. As of right now, it would take you 2.5 days to watch all the Marvel movies back to back!

First Asian woman to win Best Actress at the Oscars

MICHELLE YEOH

Malaysian-born Michelle Yeoh made Oscar history at the 2023 Academy Awards, becoming the first Asian woman to win the award for Best Actress. Yeoh won the Oscar for her role in *Everything Everywhere All at Once*, in which she plays a middle-aged Chinese American laundromat owner who gains superpowers and experiences different lives in multiple parallel universes. The adventure-packed film is at once funny and charming, with Yeoh performing most of her own stunts. At the awards, Yeoh accepted her Oscar with an emotional speech that included these words: "For all the little boys and girls who look like me watching tonight, this is proof that dreams do come true."

Youngest actress nominated for an Oscar

QUVENZHANÉ WALLIS

At nine years old, Quvenzhané Wallis became the youngest-ever Academy Award nominee for Best Actress. She received the nomination in 2013 for her role as Hushpuppy in *Beasts of the Southern Wild*. Although Wallis did not win the Oscar, she went on to gain forty-one more nominations and win twenty-four acting honors at various industry awards shows. In 2015, she received a Golden Globe Best Actress nomination for her role in *Annie*. Wallis was five years old when she auditioned for Hushpuppy, and she won the part over more than four thousand other candidates.

BILLIE EILISH

Twenty-two-year-old musician Billie Eilish has made history, becoming the youngest person ever to win two Oscars. In 2024, Eilish and her older brother, Finneas O'Connell, won Best Original Song at the Academy Awards for "What Was I Made For?" from the *Barbie* soundtrack. Previously, the sibling duo earned a first Oscar together in 2022, also for Best Original Song, for "No Time to Die" from the James Bond film of the same name. Aside from her Oscar wins, Billie Eilish has won nine Grammy Awards and was nominated for seven Grammys in 2025.

Top-earning actress

MARGOT ROBBIE

In March 2024, *Forbes* named Australian actress Margot Robbie the world's highest-paid actress of 2023, with earnings of $59 million. Robbie was also 2024's top-earning actress, thanks to her role as "stereotypical Barbie" in Greta Gerwig's *Barbie*. Her salary for the role was $12.5 million, but as a producer on the film, Robbie also earned a cut of the box office take, which was nearly $1.5 billion worldwide. Since arriving in the US in the 2010s, Robbie has starred in movies by directors Gerwig, Martin Scorsese, Wes Anderson, and Quentin Tarantino, in roles alongside Scarlett Johansson, Leonardo DiCaprio, Brad Pitt, Viola Davis, Christian Bale, and—in *Barbie*—Ryan Gosling and America Ferrera.

ADAM SANDLER

The highest-paid actor of 2023 and now 2024, according to *Forbes*, was Adam Sandler. His $73 million earnings are largely attributed to a revenue of $250 million from a four-picture deal he made in 2014 with the streaming service Netflix, which was extended in 2020 to four more movies (for an undisclosed sum). The eight movies continue to draw huge viewership figures. The site also streams movies made by Sandler's own film production company, Happy Madison Productions, among them the 2023 hits *Murder Mystery 2, You Are So Not Invited to My Bat Mitzvah*, and *Leo*, an animated musical in which Sandler gives voice to a seventy-four-year-old lizard. A portion of the star's income also came from *Adam Sandler: Love You*, the exclusive Netflix comedy special he released this year.

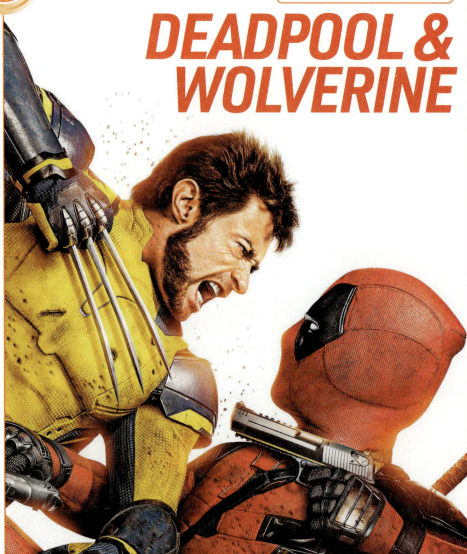

Top-grossing movie

DEADPOOL & WOLVERINE

The much-anticipated *Deadpool & Wolverine* made a splash in the US box office in July 2024. The action movie starring Ryan Reynolds and Hugh Jackman amassed $636 million dollars in the first few months alone. The film also did wonders for the Walt Disney Company as a whole. With *Deadpool & Wolverine* released in the same month as *Inside Out 2*, another smash hit, Walt Disney's finances are better than ever. The success proves that Disney films have not lost their magic touch in the box office. Bob Iger, Disney chief executive, hailed the end of 2024 as "one of the best quarters in the history of our film studio."

DESPICABLE ME

The Despicable Me movies are officially the highest-grossing animated film franchise of all time, amassing $5 billion in total. Following the 2022 release of *Minions: The Rise of Gru*, the franchise had a global total of $46.64 billion, but their new 2024 film, *Despicable Me 4*, sent the film series over the edge. It had earnings of $969 million worldwide, making it the third-highest-grossing film of 2024. The 2015 spin-off, *Minions*, is the most profitable animated film in Universal Studios' history and was the highest-grossing animated film of the year, while *Despicable Me 3* and Oscar-nominated *Despicable Me 2* hit no. 2 in their respective years of release.

Longest-running Broadway show

THE PHANTOM OF THE OPERA

Marking the end of an impressive thirty-five years on Broadway, the cast of Andrew Lloyd Webber's *The Phantom of the Opera* made its last appearance on April 16, 2023. The show had been performed 13,981 times, making it the longest-running Broadway show ever. The story, based on a novel published in 1910 by French author Gaston Leroux, tells the tragic tale of The Phantom and his love for an opera singer, Christine.

THE LION KING

Since opening on November 13, 1997, *The Lion King* musical has earned more than $9 billion. It's Broadway's third-longest-running production and is an adaptation of the hugely popular Disney animated film. Along with hit songs from the movie such as "Circle of Life" and "Hakuna Matata," the show includes new compositions by South African composer Lebo M and others. The Broadway show features songs in six African languages, including Swahili and Congolese. Since it opened, *The Lion King* has attracted audiences totaling more than 100 million people.

Musical with the most Tony Award nominations

HAMILTON

Lin-Manuel Miranda's musical biography of Founding Father Alexander Hamilton racked up sixteen Tony Award nominations to unseat the previous record holders, *The Producers* and *Billy Elliot: The Musical*, both of which had fifteen. The megahit hip-hop musical, which was inspired by historian Ron Chernow's biography of the first Secretary of the Treasury, portrays the Founding Fathers of the United States engaging in rap battles over issues such as the national debt and the French Revolution. *Hamilton* won eleven Tonys at the 2016 ceremony—one shy of *The Producers*, which retains the record for most Tony wins with twelve. *Hamilton's* Broadway success paved the way for the show to open in Chicago in 2016, with a touring show and a London production following in 2017.

ELEANOR WORTHINGTON-COX
CLEO DEMETRIOU
KERRY INGRAM
SOPHIA KIELY

In 2012, four actresses shared an Olivier Award for their roles in the British production of *Matilda*. Eleanor Worthington-Cox, Cleo Demetriou, Kerry Ingram, and Sophia Kiely all won the award for Best Actress in a Musical. Of the four actresses, Worthington-Cox, age ten, was the youngest by a few weeks. Each actress portraying *Matilda* performs two shows a week. In the United States, the four *Matilda* actresses won a special Tony Honors for Excellence in the Theatre in 2013. *Matilda*, inspired by the book by Roald Dahl, won a record seven Olivier Awards in 2012.

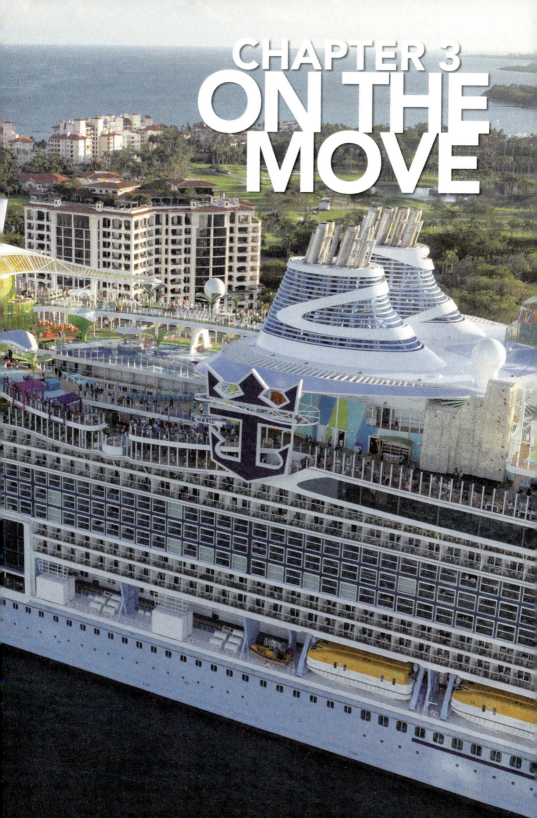

DRIVING FORCE AI TAKES THE WHEEL

The world's first-ever race featuring AI-driven cars took place in April 2024 at the Abu Dhabi Autonomous Racing League (A2RL). Four teams qualified for the final at Dubai's Yas Marina Circuit. Spectators were not impressed! The vehicles spun in circles, jerked around, and crashed, forcing a restart. While the race was an important first, it was clear that AI-driven vehicles aren't yet ready to compete professionally.

WACKY RACERS WORLD'S WEIRDEST CAR MUSEUM

A strange new world record was registered with Guinness in 2024—the Sudha Cars Museum in Hyderabad, India, has the largest collection of wacky vehicles in a museum. The cars are built by the museum's founder, Sudhakar Kanyaboyina, and are shaped like everyday objects: sports balls, types of shoes, vintage computers, and even hamburgers! Altogether Kanyaboyina has crafted around sixty of these cars, which he says take up to a year to build, and he occasionally drives them around the streets of Hyderabad.

ASTRO-STROLL SPACEX POLARIS DAWN

The first-ever civilian space walk took place in 2024, as billionaire CEO Jared Isaacman and SpaceX's Sarah Gillis exited SpaceX's Polaris Dawn spacecraft during the privately funded mission. All four civilian crew members were exposed to the elements of space when the spacecraft's hatch was opened, but only Isaacman and Gillis went out, wearing new "slimmed-down" SpaceX suits.

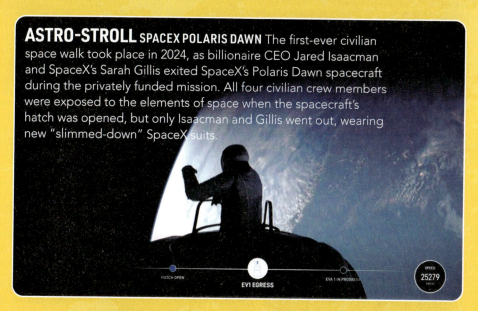

HATCH OPEN   EV1 EGRESS   EVA 1 IN PROGRESS

SPEED 25279 KM/H

STRANDED IN SPACE ASTRONAUTS

STUCK AT THE ISS NASA astronauts Suni Williams and Butch Wilmore were expecting to be in space for only eight days when they took off from Florida in June 2024. At the end of the year, they were still there, after technical issues with their spacecraft left them stranded at the International Space Station. Despite the situation, the two seemed to be in good spirits in videos and Instagram posts from the ISS. They finally returned to Earth on March 18, 2025.

EXPOSED IN THE AIR PLANE PANEL'S

SHOCKING SAFETY ISSUE Passengers on board an Alaska Airlines flight from Portland, Oregon, were in for a huge shock in January 2024 when a panel flew off their Boeing 737 Max 9, exposing the cabin to the elements. The accident took place less than ten minutes into the journey, and the plane was able to land safely with no injuries to passengers. Boeing's popularity took a big hit from the incident.

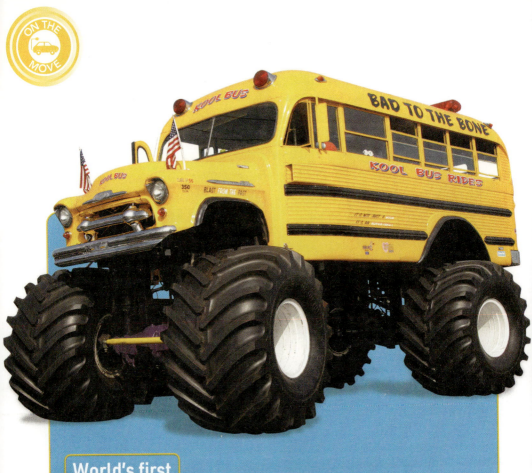

World's first

MONSTER
SCHOOL BUS

Bad to the Bone is the first monster school bus in the world. This revamped 1956 yellow bus is 13 feet tall, thanks to massive tires with 25-inch rims. The oversize bus weighs 19,000 pounds and is a favorite ride at charity events in California. But don't expect to get anywhere in a hurry—this "Kool Bus" is not built for speed and goes a maximum of just 7 miles per hour.

ROLLS-ROYCE DROPTAIL

In 2023, Rolls-Royce unveiled its new Droptail model, a luxury two-seat roadster. The first of four customized Droptails, it was named La Rose Noire for the Black Baccara rose that provided inspiration for the car's color and design. In 2024, it was the world's most-expensive street-legal car at $32 million. Its twin-turbocharged 6.75-liter V-12 engine delivers 593 horsepower—which is a lot of power, but nowhere near what some modern supercars offer. The car's elegant styling combines old-world craftsmanship with modern technology. More than 1,600 pieces of black sycamore wood veneer were painstakingly assembled by a craftsperson into an abstract artwork that covers portions of the vehicle's interior, while the car's removable hardtop is made from carbon fiber and electrochromic glass.

MOST-EXPENSIVE MODERN STREET-LEGAL CARS
In millions of US dollars

Modern street-legal car

Car	$ millions
Rolls-Royce Rose Noire Droptail	$32
Rolls-Royce Boat Tail	$28
Pagani Zonda HP Barchetta	$18.5
Bugatti La Voiture Noire	$16
Rolls-Royce Sweptail	$12.8

$ millions: 3 6 9 12 15 18 21 24 27 30

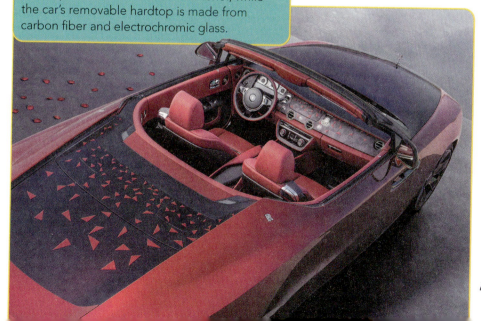

Largest cruise ship

ICON OF THE SEAS

Royal Caribbean's *Icon of the Seas*, which took its maiden voyage in January 2024, holds the record for the biggest cruise ship in the world. At 1,196 feet long and 219 feet wide, the ship can accommodate an amazing 5,610 guests and 2,350 crew members. This is not the only record held by the ship: It's also home to the world's largest water park at sea, Category 6, which includes the tallest waterslide at sea (Frightening Bolt, with a 46-foot drop) and the first-ever family raft ride at sea (the 425-foot-long Hurricane Hunter). *Icon of the Seas* reportedly cost $2 billion to build.

QTVAN

The tiny QTvan is just over 7 feet long, 2.5 feet wide, and 5 feet tall. Inside, however, it has a full-size bed for one, a kettle for boiling water, and a 19-inch TV. Britain's Environmental Transport Association (ETA) sponsored the invention of the minitrailer, which was designed to be pulled by a mobility scooter. The ETA recommends the QTvan for short trips only, since mobility scooters have a top speed of 6 miles per hour, at best.

Fastest land vehicle

THRUST SSC

The world's fastest car is the Thrust SSC, which reached a speed of 763 miles per hour on October 15, 1997, in the Black Rock Desert of Nevada. SSC stands for supersonic (faster than the speed of sound) car. The Thrust SSC's amazing speed comes from two jet engines with 110,000 brake horsepower. That's as much as 145 Formula 1 race cars. The British-made car uses about 5 gallons of jet fuel in one second and takes just five seconds to reach its top speed. At that speed, the Thrust SSC could travel from New York City to San Francisco in less than four hours. Another British manufacturer is developing a new supersonic car, the Bloodhound, with a projected speed of 1,000 miles per hour. If it reaches that, it will set a new world record.

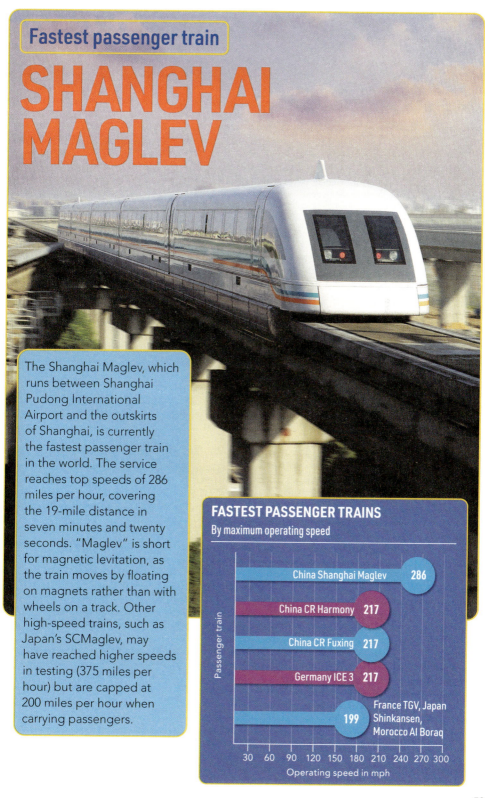

SHANGHAI MAGLEV

The Shanghai Maglev, which runs between Shanghai Pudong International Airport and the outskirts of Shanghai, is currently the fastest passenger train in the world. The service reaches top speeds of 286 miles per hour, covering the 19-mile distance in seven minutes and twenty seconds. "Maglev" is short for magnetic levitation, as the train moves by floating on magnets rather than with wheels on a track. Other high-speed trains, such as Japan's SCMaglev, may have reached higher speeds in testing (375 miles per hour) but are capped at 200 miles per hour when carrying passengers.

FASTEST PASSENGER TRAINS
By maximum operating speed

Passenger train	Operating speed in mph
China Shanghai Maglev	286
China CR Harmony	217
China CR Fuxing	217
Germany ICE 3	217
France TGV, Japan Shinkansen, Morocco Al Boraq	199

Operating speed in mph: 30 60 90 120 150 180 210 240 270 300

Fastest unpiloted plane

X-43A

In November 2004, NASA launched its experimental X-43A plane for a test flight over the Pacific Ocean. The X-43A plane reached Mach 9.6, which is more than nine times the speed of sound and nearly 7,000 miles per hour. A B-52 aircraft carried the X-43A and a Pegasus rocket booster into the air, releasing them at 40,000 feet. At that point, the booster—essentially a fuel-packed engine—ignited, blasting the unpiloted X-43A higher and faster, before separating from the plane. The plane continued to fly for several minutes at 110,000 feet, before crashing (intentionally) into the ocean.

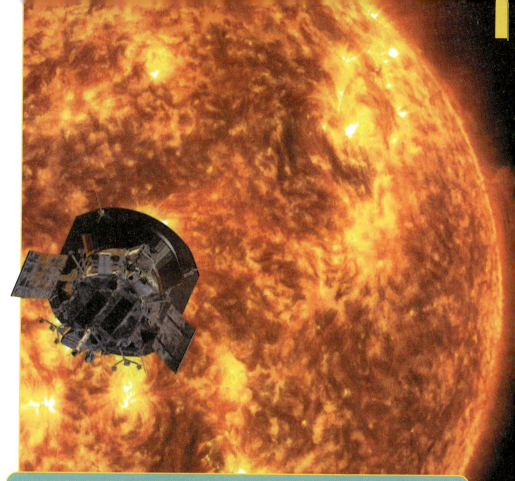

In December 2024, the Parker Solar Probe set a new record for the fastest known human-made object, traveling at up to 430,000 miles per hour. At that speed you could fly from New York to San Francisco in less than 30 seconds! Jointly operated by NASA and Johns Hopkins University and equipped with a wide range of scientific equipment, the Parker Solar Probe is on a seven-year mission to study the sun's atmosphere. Withstanding extreme heat and radiation, it sends data and images back to Earth, revolutionizing our understanding of the star at the heart of our solar system. The probe shattered a second record in December 2024, reaching a distance of just 3.8 million miles from the solar surface—the closest a spacecraft has ever been to the sun.

Fastest human-made object

PARKER SOLAR PROBE

Fastest piloted spacecraft

APOLLO 10

NASA's Apollo 10 spacecraft reached its top speed on its descent to Earth, hurtling through the atmosphere at 24,816 miles per hour and splashing down on May 26, 1969. The spacecraft's crew had traveled faster than anyone on Earth. The mission was a dress rehearsal for the first moon landing by Apollo 11, two months later. The Apollo 10 spacecraft consisted of a Command and Service Module, called Charlie Brown, and a Lunar Module, called Snoopy. Today, Charlie Brown is on display at the Science Museum in London, England.

Snoopy
The Apollo 10 crew launched Snoopy toward the moon to examine its surface.

APOLLO 10

05/18/1969
Launch date

12:49 p.m.
EDT Launch

05/21/1969
Date entered lunar orbit

192:03:23
Duration of mission: 192 hours, 3 minutes, 23 seconds

05/26/1969
Return date

12:52 p.m.
EDT Splashdown

Charlie Brown
Following a successful eight-day mission, Charlie Brown splashed down 400 miles east of American Samoa in the South Pacific Ocean.

LIFTOFF

The Apollo 10 spacecraft was launched from Florida's Cape Canaveral, known as Cape Kennedy at the time. It was the fourth crewed Apollo launch in seven months.

FORMULA ROSSA

Fastest roller coaster

Thrill seekers hurtle along the Formula Rossa track at 149.1 miles per hour. The high-speed roller coaster is part of Ferrari World in Abu Dhabi, United Arab Emirates. Ferrari World also features the world's largest indoor theme park, at 1.5 million square feet. The Formula Rossa roller-coaster seats are red Ferrari-shaped cars that travel from 0 to 62 miles per hour in just two seconds—as fast as a race car. The ride's g-force is so extreme that passengers must wear goggles to protect their eyes. G-force acts on a body due to acceleration and gravity. People can withstand 6 to 8 g's for short periods. The Formula Rossa g-force is 4.8 g's during acceleration and 1.7 g's at maximum speed.

FORMULA ROSSA WORLD RECORDS

149.1 mph
Speed

1.7 g's
G-force

4.8 g's
Acceleration

Rising 86 feet above Six Flags Hurricane Harbor Chicago amusement park, Tsunami Surge is the tallest water coaster in the world. Psychedelic visual effects light the way as thrill seekers are blasted through 950 feet of slides, tunnels, and hairpin bends at top speeds of 28 miles per hour. This attraction—the twenty-fifth to debut at the Six Flags park—uses the latest technology in jet propulsion to power its passengers all the way up the steepest slopes . . . and down again.

Tallest water coaster

TSUNAMI SURGE

CHAPTER 4
SUPER STRUCTURES

SUPER STRUCTURES
trending

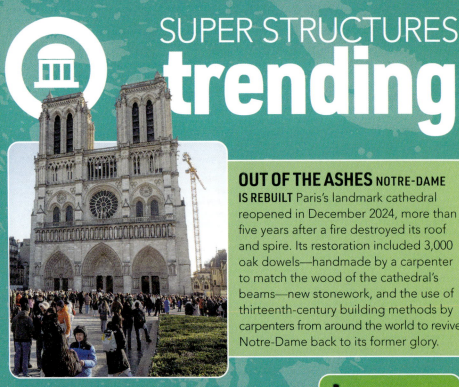

OUT OF THE ASHES NOTRE-DAME IS REBUILT

Paris's landmark cathedral reopened in December 2024, more than five years after a fire destroyed its roof and spire. Its restoration included 3,000 oak dowels—handmade by a carpenter to match the wood of the cathedral's beams—new stonework, and the use of thirteenth-century building methods by carpenters from around the world to revive Notre-Dame back to its former glory.

SO BRAT CHARLI XCX GREEN GOES VIRAL

An unexpected color showed up in the interior design world in 2024, as Charli XCX's iconic "brat green" found its way into even the chicest circles. The shade, immortalized on *Brat*'s album cover, is a bold lime green that the singer has admitted was a deliberately controversial choice. In 2024, it was everywhere, from high-fashion campaigns to accent walls in designers' homes.

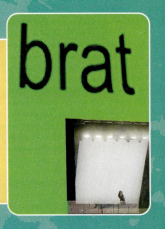

LOST CITY MAYA CITY DISCOVERED WITH LASERS

Tulane PhD student Luke Auld-Thomas made a huge discovery in 2024 while examining lidar survey maps published by the Mexican government. The lidar survey works by firing laser pulses at the ground from a plane and mapping what is below based on how long it takes for the signal to return. In one map, Auld-Thomas spotted the remains of a major city hidden in a Mexican jungle. He and his colleagues discovered temple pyramids, a reservoir, and 6,764 buildings in the ancient city, which they named Valeriana.

SWEET SOLUTIONS

STARBUCKS' JAPANESE ECO-CAFE Starbucks announced a new building project in 2024. The coffee giant is teaming up with Japanese brewery Kirishima Shuzo to create a café powered by sweet potatoes! The eco-friendly Starbucks in Miyakonojo city will be run on biogas converted from the brewery's potato scraps (left over from brewing the spirit *shochu*). Built from energy-efficient materials, the café is due to open in spring 2026.

DEADLY CRASH BALTIMORE BRIDGE

COLLAPSES A terrible crash took down Baltimore's Francis Scott Key Bridge in March 2024, when a shipping container struck one of the bridge's pillars. The cargo ship *Dali*, which weighed more than 100,000 tons, had lost power and sent out a Mayday call indicating that the crew had lost control of the ship. The impact of the collision caused the bridge to collapse around the cargo, completely blocking access to the Port of Baltimore.

SUPER STRUCTURES

HONG KONG

Hong Kong, China, has 558 buildings that reach 492 feet or higher, six of which are actually 1,000 feet or higher. The tallest three are the International Commerce Centre (ICC) at 1,588 feet, Two International Finance Centre at 1,352 feet, and Central Plaza at 1,227 feet. Hong Kong's stunning skyline towers above Victoria Harbour. Most of its tallest buildings are on Hong Kong Island, although the other side of the harbor, Kowloon, is growing. Every night a light, laser, and sound show called "A Symphony of Lights" illuminates the sky against a backdrop of about forty of Hong Kong's skyscrapers.

NUMBER OF SKYSCRAPERS AT 492 FEET OR HIGHER, 2024

- Hong Kong, China
- Shenzhen, China
- New York City, US
- Dubai, United Arab Emirates

Height in feet

600
540
480
420
360
300
240
180
120
60

558
414
318
263

Number of skyscrapers

World's largest soccer stadium
RUNGRADO

It took over two years to build Rungrado 1st of May Stadium, a huge sports venue with a capacity for up to 150,000 people. The 197-foot-tall stadium opened in 1989 on Rungra Island in North Korea's capital, Pyongyang. The stadium hosts international soccer matches on its natural grass pitch and has other facilities such as an indoor swimming pool, training halls, and a 1,312-foot rubberized running track. Following a remodel in 2014, some estimate that the stadium's capacity is now 114,000; even so, there is no other soccer (or as the rest of the world would say, *football*) stadium that can host more spectators.

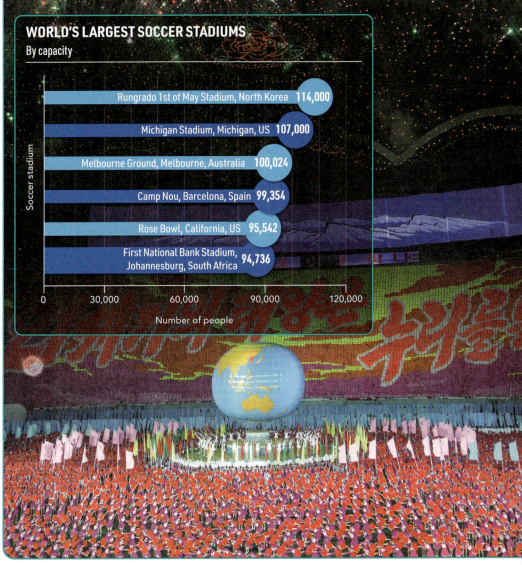

WORLD'S LARGEST SOCCER STADIUMS
By capacity

Soccer stadium

Rungrado 1st of May Stadium, North Korea	114,000
Michigan Stadium, Michigan, US	107,000
Melbourne Ground, Melbourne, Australia	100,024
Camp Nou, Barcelona, Spain	99,354
Rose Bowl, California, US	95,542
First National Bank Stadium, Johannesburg, South Africa	94,736

0   30,000   60,000   90,000   120,000

Number of people

Most fairy-tale castle

NEUSCHWANSTEIN

Neuschwanstein Castle, in the Bavarian Alps within Germany, is also known as the Fairy-Tale Castle, or "Castle of the Fairy-Tale King." It is thought to have been the inspiration for the castle in Disney's *Sleeping Beauty*. Built by King Ludwig II of Bavaria in the late-nineteenth century, Neuschwanstein is known for its impressive Alpine setting, its white limestone walls, and blue turrets. The castle is an idealized version of those built in the medieval period and reflects Ludwig II's extravagant taste and interest in medieval romances. The so-called Fairy-Tale King died before Neuschwanstein was finished being built.

MALBORK

The biggest castle in the world by land area is Poland's Malbork Castle, which occupies more than 52 acres on the banks of the Nogat River near Gdańsk. The castle is actually a huge fortress complex of three separate redbrick castles. A religious order called the Teutonic Knights started building the castle in 1274, and the complex reached its current extent in 1406. Europe was turbulent in the Middle Ages, and the knights often found themselves defending the castle against armies from Poland and Lithuania. The knights lost a decisive battle in 1410, and Malbork Castle fell to the Poles, becoming a royal residence in 1466. Today, more than 700,000 people visit the complex every year.

World's tallest building

BURJ KHALIFA

Laid end to end, the steel used here would stretch one quarter of the way around the world!

Holding the record for the world's tallest building since January 2010, the Burj Khalifa is 2,716.5 feet tall. It not only qualifies as the world's tallest building, but also as the tallest human-made structure and the tallest freestanding structure. It also has the largest number of stories and the highest aluminum-and-glass facades (which incidentally cover the same area as twenty-five football fields). The tower took six years to build, with 12,000 men on-site day after day, completing 22 million hours of work. Dubbed a "vertical city," the tower holds around 10,000 people at any given time.

TOUGH CLIMB

No fewer than 2,909 steps lead up to floor 160 of the Burj Khalifa. Anyone wishing to go higher has to do so climbing ladders.

DUBAI'S BURJ KHALIFA WORLD RECORDS

1,654 feet
Tallest elevator inside a building

163
Number of floors

1,448 feet
Highest restaurant from ground level

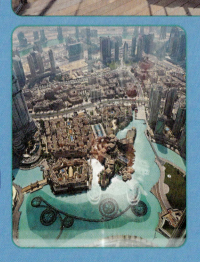

GOING UP

SUPER STRUCTURES

Opal capital of the world

COOBER PEDY

Some 60 percent of this Australian mining town's approximately 2,500 residents live in cave-like homes that are dug into the ground, not constructed above it. The region's scalding summer temperatures are the reason for these unusual homes. Surface temperatures in Coober Pedy often climb above 120°F, but belowground, temperatures remain comfortably in the mid-70s year-round. Called the opal capital of the world—the majority of Earth's opals come from this area—Coober Pedy also has underground churches, museums, hotel rooms, and campsites. The region's sandstone is structurally sound but also relatively easy to carve away—when Coober Pedy's subterranean homeowners want extra living space, they simply dig out new rooms for themselves.

World's largest swimming pool
CITYSTARS

Citystars Sharm El Sheikh lagoon in Egypt stretches over 29.7 acres. It was created by Crystal Lagoons, the same company that built the former record holder at San Alfonso del Mar in Chile. The lagoon at Sharm El Sheikh cost $5.5 million to create and is designed to be sustainable, using salt water from local underground aquifers. The creators purify this water not just for recreation, but also to provide clean, fresh water to the surrounding community.

LARGEST SWIMMING POOLS
Size in acres

Swimming pool

- Citystars Sharm El Sheikh, Egypt **29.7**
- San Alfonso del Mar, Algarrobo, Chile **19**
- MahaSamutr, Hua Hin, Thailand **17.8**
- **10** Diamante, Cabo San Lucas, Mexico
- **5** Las Brisas, Chile

Acres: 3 6 9 12 15 18 21 24 27 30

Crossing the floodplain of China's Yangtze River, a terrain of hills, lakes, flatlands, and rice paddies, the 102-mile-long Danyang-Kunshan Grand Bridge is the longest bridge in the world. It is a viaduct, which means it is built using many short spans rather than one long one. The spans are raised 328 feet above the ground, on average, and are supported on 2,000 reinforced cement concrete pillars. It's a design that helps the high-speed rail bridge to cross the ever-changing landscape between the Chinese cities of Shanghai and Nanjing. Costing $8.5 billion to construct, the bridge took four years to build using a task force of 10,000 laborers.

World's longest bridge

DANYANG-
KUNSHAN
GRAND BRIDGE

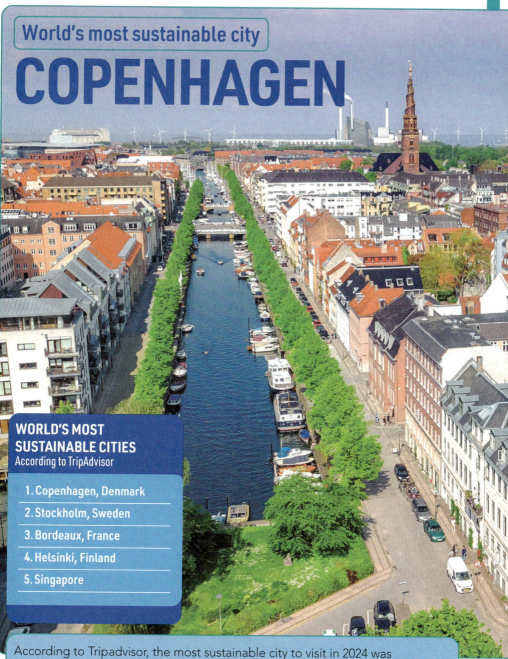

World's most sustainable city

COPENHAGEN

WORLD'S MOST SUSTAINABLE CITIES
According to TripAdvisor

1. Copenhagen, Denmark
2. Stockholm, Sweden
3. Bordeaux, France
4. Helsinki, Finland
5. Singapore

According to Tripadvisor, the most sustainable city to visit in 2024 was Copenhagen, Denmark! Tripadvisor partnered with the Global Destination Sustainability Movement to judge the top places for green living. Copenhagen scored points for its nearly 340 miles of bike paths, eco-friendly hotels, and organic food. A huge percentage of energy in Denmark comes from wind power, and the capital is known for its use of electric buses and waste-to-energy plant—all showing the city's commitment to renewable energy as part of its plan to be carbon neutral by 2025.

KHALIFA AVENUE
QATAR

Completed in 2020, the Khalifa Avenue living wall in Doha, Qatar, features more than 75,000 square feet of lush plant life situated on nearly vertical surfaces along the sides of an elevated roadway. That's a green space significantly larger than a football field—but unlike a football field, this greenery is growing on a wall. Qatari company Nakheel Landscapes installed the wall using the ANS Living Wall System pioneered by British company ANS Global. Living walls—also known as green walls or vertical gardens—not only look beautiful but also improve air quality in urban areas. One challenge for Khalifa Avenue's builders is that local temperatures regularly climb above 120°F in the summer, which is much too hot for many plants.

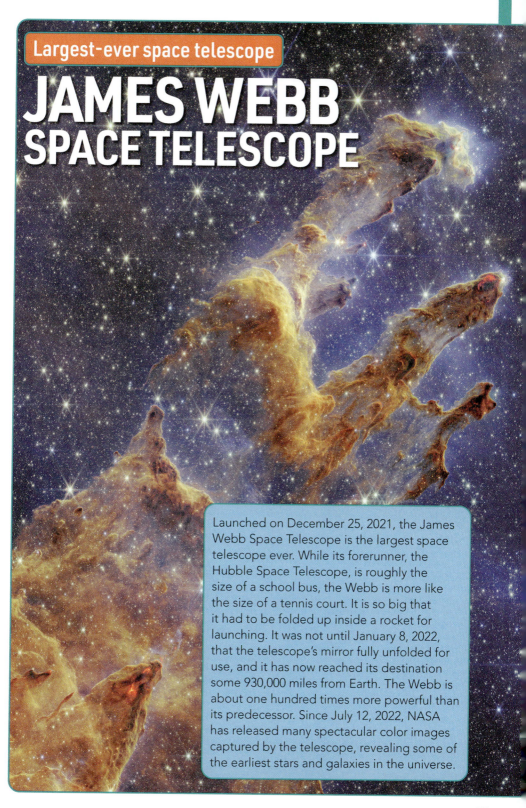

JAMES WEBB SPACE TELESCOPE

Launched on December 25, 2021, the James Webb Space Telescope is the largest space telescope ever. While its forerunner, the Hubble Space Telescope, is roughly the size of a school bus, the Webb is more like the size of a tennis court. It is so big that it had to be folded up inside a rocket for launching. It was not until January 8, 2022, that the telescope's mirror fully unfolded for use, and it has now reached its destination some 930,000 miles from Earth. The Webb is about one hundred times more powerful than its predecessor. Since July 12, 2022, NASA has released many spectacular color images captured by the telescope, revealing some of the earliest stars and galaxies in the universe.

World's largest tomb of a known individual

QIN SHI HUANG'S TOMB

Emperor Qin Shi Huang ruled China in the third century BCE. In 1974, people digging a well in the fields northeast of Xi'an, in Shaanxi province, accidentally discovered the ancient tomb. Further investigation revealed a burial complex of over 20 square miles. A large pit contained 6,000 life-size terra-cotta warrior figures, each one different from the next and dressed according to rank. A second and third pit contained 2,000 more figures; clay horses; about 40,000 bronze weapons; and other artifacts. Historians think that as many as 700,000 people worked for about thirty-six years to create this incredible mausoleum. The emperor's tomb remains sealed to preserve its contents and to protect workers from possible hazards, such as chemical poisoning from mercury in the surrounding soil.

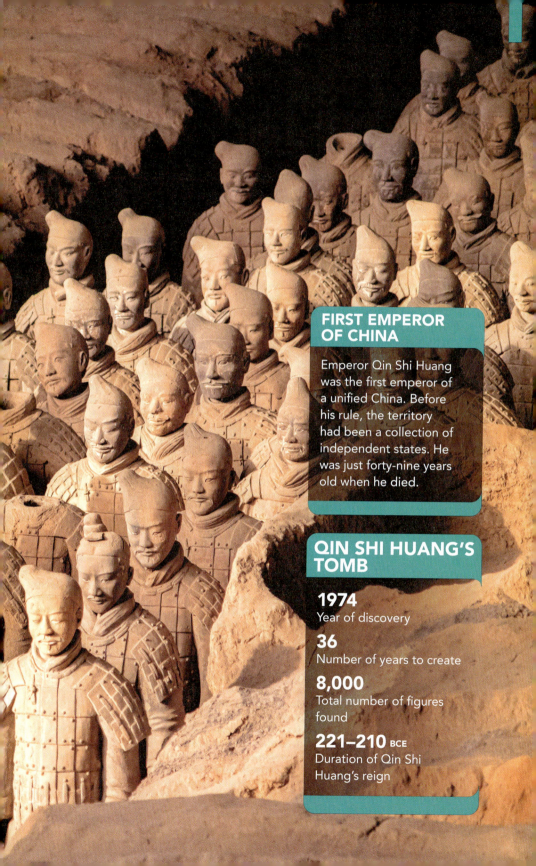

FIRST EMPEROR OF CHINA

Emperor Qin Shi Huang was the first emperor of a unified China. Before his rule, the territory had been a collection of independent states. He was just forty-nine years old when he died.

QIN SHI HUANG'S TOMB

1974
Year of discovery

36
Number of years to create

8,000
Total number of figures found

221–210 BCE
Duration of Qin Shi Huang's reign

Largest playing card structure

KOLKATA, INDIA

In 2023, fifteen-year-old Arnav Daga set a new record for the world's largest structure built from playing cards. The teenager used an amazing 143,000 cards to recreate buildings from Kolkata, India, where he lived. He spent forty-one days stacking the cards in order to create the massive masterpiece, measuring 40 feet in length; 11 feet, 4 inches in height; and 16 feet, 8 inches in width. One building, the Shaheed Minar, gave Daga particular trouble, as his cards kept falling down while he tried to recreate it.

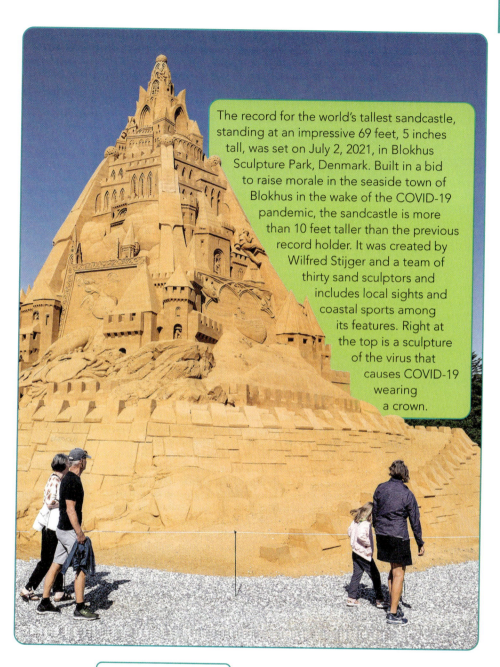

The record for the world's tallest sandcastle, standing at an impressive 69 feet, 5 inches tall, was set on July 2, 2021, in Blokhus Sculpture Park, Denmark. Built in a bid to raise morale in the seaside town of Blokhus in the wake of the COVID-19 pandemic, the sandcastle is more than 10 feet taller than the previous record holder. It was created by Wilfred Stijger and a team of thirty sand sculptors and includes local sights and coastal sports among its features. Right at the top is a sculpture of the virus that causes COVID-19 wearing a crown.

World's tallest sandcastle

BLOKHUS SCULPTURE PARK DENMARK

World's longest LEGO® ship

WORLD DREAM

In 2017, 1,000 cruise passengers and volunteers came together to help build a replica of the *World Dream* cruise ship, a vessel owned by China's Dream Cruises Management Ltd. Boasting more than 2.5 million LEGO blocks, this spectacle is the longest LEGO ship ever built. It's a complete scaled-down replica of the *World Dream* cruise ship, with all eighteen of its decks, and measures 27 feet, 8.5 inches in length. Upon completion, it was placed in Hong Kong's Kai Tak Cruise Terminal for all to see.

World's largest sculpture cut from a single piece of stone

SPHINX

The Great Sphinx stands guard near three large pyramids in Giza, Egypt. Historians believe ancient people created the sculpture about 4,500 years ago for the pharaoh Khafre. They carved the sphinx from one mass of limestone in the desert floor, creating a sculpture about 66 feet high and 240 feet long. It has the head of a pharaoh and the body of a lion. The sculpture may represent Ruti, a twin lion god from ancient myths that protected the sun god, Ra, and guarded entrances to the underworld. Sand has covered and preserved the Great Sphinx, but over many years, wind and humidity have worn parts of the soft limestone away, some of which have been restored using blocks of sand and quicklime.

GREAT SPHINX

4,500 years
Estimated age

240 feet
Length

66 feet
Height

CHAPTER 5
HIGH TECH

CUTE PAIR **A PENGUIN AND EGG IN SPACE** A stunning image captured by the James Webb Space Telescope in July 2024 shows a pair of intertwining galaxies—one an elliptical galaxy and the other a spiral galaxy—which collectively are called ARP 142. But scientists have given the galaxies a far catchier nickname: the Penguin and the Egg. The two galaxies are approximately 100,000 light-years apart, which might seem like a vast distance, but in astronomical terms, that virtually makes them next-door neighbors.

FROM LOO TO LIFTOFF **JET FUEL FROM HUMAN WASTE** In April 2024, biofuel company Firefly announced that it will build the world's first commercial factory to make jet fuel from human poo in Essex, England. The company also announced that it had come to an agreement with aviation company Wizz Air to produce 525,000 tons of sustainable aviation fuel (SAF) over the next fifteen years.

RECYCLED PEE *DUNE*-INSPIRED SPACE SUIT As NASA seeks to expand its lunar program, it is anticipated that astronauts may need to spend up to twenty-four hours a week performing space walks. Currently, astronauts can carry only up to 2 pints of water in their space suits while performing these tasks. Inspired by the still suits worn in the sci-fi epic *Dune*, scientists are working on developing a system for extracting drinkable water from urine so that astronauts can access more water during space walks.

SAY CHEESE! YEARBOOK PHOTOBOOTH One of the biggest TikTok trends of 2024 was a filter that shows people what they might look like if they were given a '90s makeover. Users select the filter, strike a pose, then tap the screen, and see their faces morphed into a yearbook portrait that mimics the headshots one might find in a high-school yearbook. The filter, which was created by TikTok user and multidisciplinary designer Joannitante, amassed around 2.6 billion views.

CALLING ALL GAMERS! NINTENDO MUSEUM OPENS IN KYOTO On October 2, 2024, Nintendo—famous for creating iconic games *Super Mario* and *The Legend of Zelda*—opened the Nintendo Museum in Kyoto, Japan. Located in a renovated factory, the museum has three zones: "Learn" is devoted to the company's 135-year history; "Experience" is a series of interactive exhibits; and in "Create and Play," visitors are invited to make their own creations.

Celebrity with the most Instagram followers

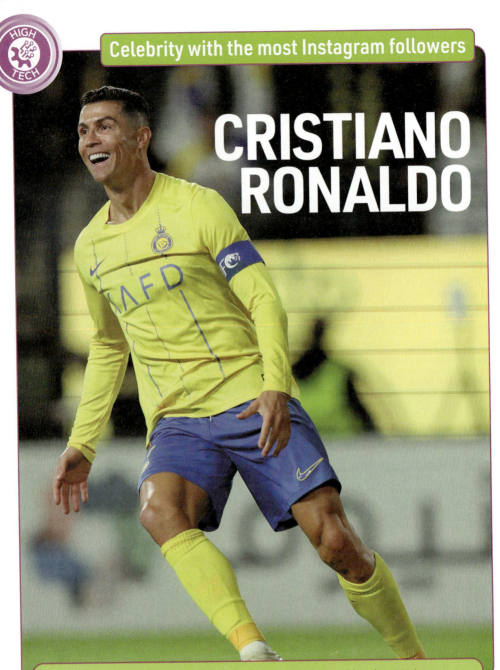

CRISTIANO RONALDO

Portuguese soccer icon Cristiano Ronaldo may once again be the year's most followed celebrity on Instagram. In February 2025, he had 648 million followers. In 2022, Ronaldo became the first player to score in five consecutive FIFA World Cups (2006–2022), and in 2023, he inspired many others to follow in his footsteps after signing with Saudi club AlNassr. As the club's new captain, he commanded an annual salary of $213 million—the highest in the world. Ronaldo's longtime rival, Lionel Messi, holds the title of second-most Instagram followers, with 505 million as of February 2025.

YUSAKU MAEZAWA

Yusaku Maezawa holds the title for most retweeted tweet of all time, with a whopping 4.4 million retweets. Celebrating his company's high Christmas–New Year earnings in 2018–2019, the Japanese billionaire posted a tweet with accompanying images promising to split one hundred million yen ($937,638) among one hundred randomly chosen people. Another giveaway from Yusaku also made the list as the third-most-retweeted tweet. The prospect of free money definitely helped motivate people to make this one go viral!

MOST-DOWNLOADED
FREE IPHONE GAME
APPS OF 2024

1. *Block Blast!*

2. *Monopoly Go!*

3. *Roblox*

4. *Call of Duty: Warzone Mobile*

5. *Township*

Most-downloaded free
iPhone game app of 2024

BLOCK BLAST!

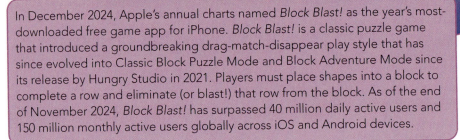

In December 2024, Apple's annual charts named *Block Blast!* as the year's most-downloaded free game app for iPhone. *Block Blast!* is a classic puzzle game that introduced a groundbreaking drag-match-disappear play style that has since evolved into Classic Block Puzzle Mode and Block Adventure Mode since its release by Hungry Studio in 2021. Players must place shapes into a block to complete a row and eliminate (or blast!) that row from the block. As of the end of November 2024, *Block Blast!* has surpassed 40 million daily active users and 150 million monthly active users globally across iOS and Android devices.

"BABY SHARK DANCE"

The addictive "Baby Shark Dance" video by South Korean brand Pinkfong has been viewed at least 15 billion times since its upload in June 2016, making it the most-viewed YouTube video ever. The simple song and its accompanying dance moves went viral in 2018, and the "Baby Shark Dance" now has its own line of merchandise, as well as an animated series on Nickelodeon. There is even a remix starring Luis Fonsi. This is fitting, given that Fonsi's "Despacito" held the no. 1 spot prior to "Baby Shark Dance."

YouTube account to reach 20 million subscribers fastest

CRISTIANO RONALDO

It took soccer legend Cristiano Ronaldo fewer than twenty-four hours to hit an incredible 20 million subscribers on YouTube. Ronaldo created the account "UR Cristiano" on August 21, 2024, and hit the 10 million mark in just twelve hours—unsurprising given the popularity of the star's other social media accounts. The previous fastest YouTuber to reach 10 million was MrBeast, who took 132 days. As of November 2024, Ronaldo's channel has 69.7 million subscribers watching his videos—which include a mix of comedy, life updates, and soccer commentary.

RYAN KAJI

Ryan Kaji, the star of *Ryan's World*, made $35 million in 2023, becoming the highest-earning kid on YouTube at just twelve years old! *Ryan's World* has attracted more than 38 million subscribers, with the number set to keep on growing. In 2017, Kaji became the youngest-ever person on a *Forbes* top-earners list when his channel made $11 million. At the time, he was just six! His content has changed since then, from reviewing toys to posting educational videos about his interests in the sciences, arts and crafts, and music. Videos on *Ryan's World* also feature his parents and his younger sisters, twins Emma and Kate.

Most-viewed TikTok video

ZACH KING

Proving that the world still loves watching magic, three of the five most-viewed videos on the TikTok platform come from American illusionist Zach King. The most popular TikTok video ever, with 2.3 billion views, shows King pulling off a Harry Potter–based trick in which he uses a longboard and mirrored surface to create the illusion of flying on a broomstick down a California street. The only TikToks in the top five that are *not* by King come from makeup YouTuber James Charles, with his "Sisters Christmas Party" (2019), which has 1.7 billion views, and Australian influencer Leah Halton, whose inverted filter lip-sync (2024) has more than 913 million views.

CHARLI D'AMELIO

Charli D'Amelio became the first TikTok user to hit 100 million followers on the app in November 2020, when she was only sixteen years old. The social media personality, who joined the app in 2019, quickly became known for her lip-syncing and dancing challenge videos. Her one hundred million milestone came at a controversial time, with D'Amelio losing around one million followers for her behavior in a "Dinner with the D'Amelios" YouTube segment. Despite this, D'Amelio's online presence has earned her an estimated net worth of $23.5 million, including income from movie roles and brand partnerships.

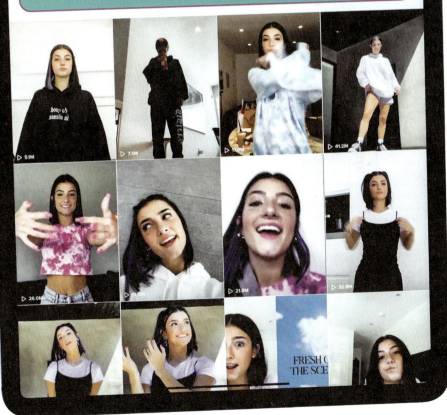

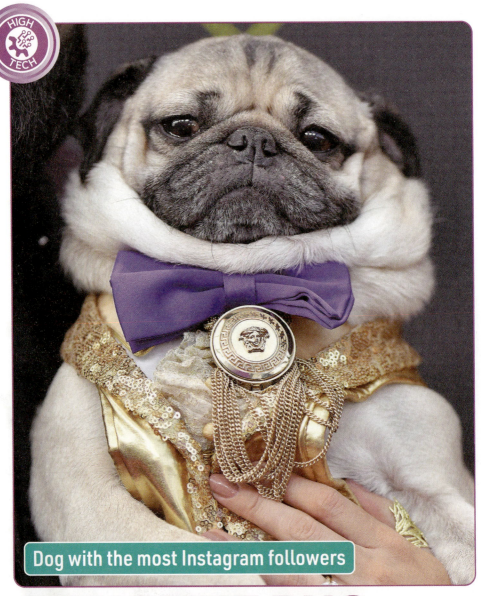

Dog with the most Instagram followers

DOUG THE PUG

With 3.6 million followers, Doug the Pug is the most popular dog on Instagram. And what a career this adorable pooch has had! Since launching his account in 2014, Doug has published a *New York Times* bestseller, won two People's Choice Awards, and met countless dog-loving celebrities. In 2020, he starred in a Super Bowl ad and he was the voice of Monchi in the movie *The Mitchells vs. the Machines* in 2021! Doug has even launched a range of natural grooming products for canines. In 2022, a very special foundation offering support to children with life-threatening illnesses was set up in Doug's name.

NALA CAT

In January 2020, and with a total of 4.3 million followers, Nala Cat broke the Guinness World Record for the cat with the most followers on Instagram. As of November 2024, the feline remains just as popular, with 4.5 million. Adopted from a shelter at just four months old, the Siamese tabby charms online viewers around the world with her bright blue eyes and supercute headgear.

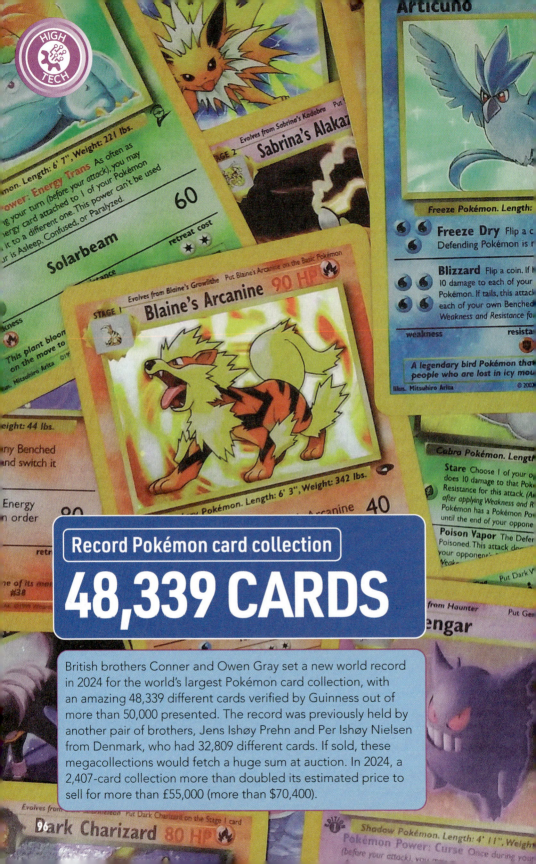

Record Pokémon card collection

48,339 CARDS

British brothers Conner and Owen Gray set a new world record in 2024 for the world's largest Pokémon card collection, with an amazing 48,339 different cards verified by Guinness out of more than 50,000 presented. The record was previously held by another pair of brothers, Jens Ishøy Prehn and Per Ishøy Nielsen from Denmark, who had 32,809 different cards. If sold, these megacollections would fetch a huge sum at auction. In 2024, a 2,407-card collection more than doubled its estimated price to sell for more than £55,000 (more than $70,400).

Best-selling video game ever

TPM
6

NEXT

TETRIS

Tetris, developed by Russian computer scientist Alexey Pajitnov in 1984, has sold over 500 million copies worldwide—more than any other game. It has been available on almost every video game console since its creation and has seen a resurgence in sales as an app for cell phones and tablets. The iconic puzzle game was the first video game to be exported from the Soviet Union to the United States and the first to be played in outer space, and is often listed as one of the best video games of all time. In 2019, Nintendo released *Tetris 99* for Nintendo Switch—a multiplayer version of the game that sees ninety-nine players compete against one another online.

ORIGIN

LINES
40

TIME
01:30

EA SPORTS
COLLEGE FOOTBALL 25

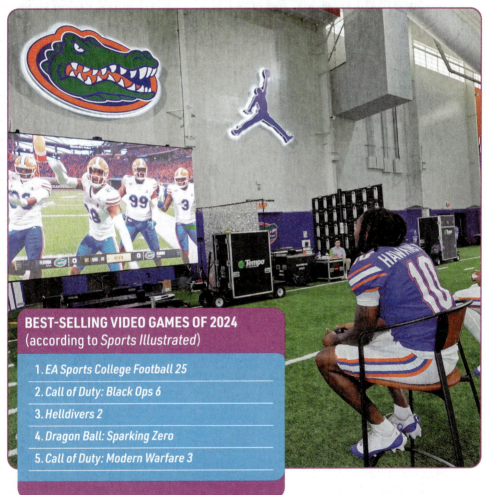

BEST-SELLING VIDEO GAMES OF 2024
(according to *Sports Illustrated*)

1. *EA Sports College Football 25*
2. *Call of Duty: Black Ops 6*
3. *Helldivers 2*
4. *Dragon Ball: Sparking Zero*
5. *Call of Duty: Modern Warfare 3*

According to *Sports Illustrated*, *EA Sports College Football 25* was the best-selling video game of 2024. Released in July 2024, *College Football* also became America's best-selling sports game of all time in November, officially taking the top spot from basketball game *NBA 2K21*. It is the first game to feature collegiate football teams in eleven years and was therefore highly anticipated. While exact figures have not been released to the general public, sales were tracked and verified by Circana, who confirmed *College Football*'s victory.

HIGH TECH

PS2

PlayStation's legendary PS2 console is still the best-selling console of all time, with parent company Sony confirming the sale of more than 158 million units. Launched in 2000, the PS2 was particularly successful because it could play PS2 games, PS1 games, and even DVDs. In second place, with around 154 million units sold, is the Nintendo DS, released in 2004 and now discontinued, and in third place is the Nintendo Switch, with more than 142 million units sold.

Best-selling video game franchise of all time

MARIO

Nintendo's *Mario* franchise has sold more than 875 million units since the first game was released in 1983. Since then, Mario; his brother, Luigi; and other characters like Princess Peach and Yoshi have become household names, starring in dozens of games. In the early games, like *Super Mario World*, players jump over obstacles, collect tokens, and capture flags as Mario journeys through the Mushroom Kingdom to save the princess. The franchise has since diversified to include other popular games such as *Mario Kart*, a racing game showcasing the inhabitants and landscapes of the Mushroom Kingdom.

MINE

According to the Guinness World Records, Minefaire 2016, a huge gathering of *Minecraft* fans, was the biggest convention ever for a single video game. Held October 15–16 at the Greater Philadelphia Expo Center in Oaks, Pennsylvania, the event attracted 12,140 people. Game developer Markus Persson created *Minecraft* in 2009 and sold it to Microsoft in 2014 for $2.5 billion. Gamers can play alone or with other players online. The game involves breaking and placing blocks to build whatever gamers can imagine—from simple constructions to huge virtual worlds. Attendance was not the only element of Minefaire to gain world-record status. On October 15, the largest-ever *Minecraft* architecture lesson attracted 342 attendees, and American gamer Lestat Wade broke the record for building the tallest staircase in *Minecraft* in one minute.

Biggest convention for a single video game

MINEFAIRE 2016

MINEFAIRE STATS

12,140
Number of people attending Minefaire

150,000
Total area, in square feet, of *Minecraft-*centered attractions

3
Number of Guinness World Records broken at the fair

Most popular new emoji

HEAD SHAKING HORIZONTALLY

The 2024 World Emoji Award for Most Popular New Emoji went to the Head Shaking Horizontally. All emojis released in the Emoji 15.1 update were eligible for the award, which is decided based on global emoji usage data. It looks like people were excited for a new way to say no, with the head shaking vertically emoji (a nod for yes) coming in second! The new phoenix emoji was the third most used from the 15.1 set, with the lime and broken chain coming in fourth and fifth, respectively. Emojis in the update that didn't make the top five include emojis for walking, running, kneeling, using a wheelchair, and walking with a cane, as well as a brown mushroom.

VERSIUS

British robot specialist Cambridge Medical Robotics developed the world's smallest surgical robot in 2017. Operated by a surgeon using a console guide with a 3D screen, the robot is able to carry out keyhole surgery. The scientists modeled the robot, called Versius, on the human arm, giving it similar wrist joints to allow maximum flexibility. Keyhole surgery involves making very small cuts on the surface of a person's body, through which a surgeon can then operate. The recovery time of the patient is usually quicker when operated on in this way.

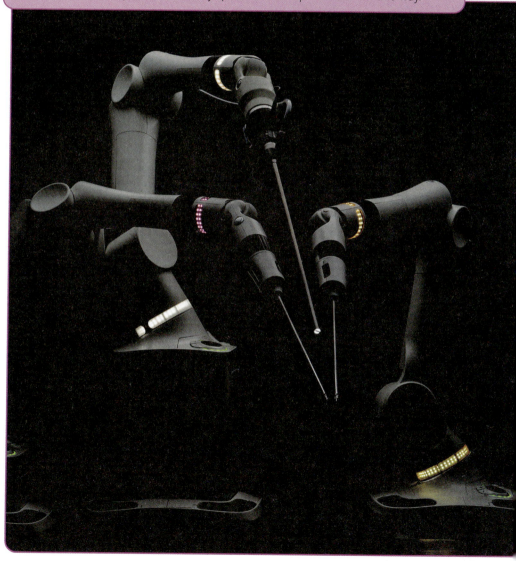

Biggest walking robot

FANNY

Fanny is a massive 26-foot-high, 51-foot-long, fire-breathing dragon. She is also the world's biggest walking robot. In 2012, a German company designed and built Fanny using both hydraulic and electronic parts. She is radio remote-controlled with nine controllers, while 238 sensors allow the robot to assess her environment. She does this while walking on her four legs or stretching wings that span 39 feet. Powered by a 140-horsepower diesel engine, Fanny weighs a hefty 24,250 pounds—as much as two elephants—and breathes real fire using 24 pounds of liquid gas.

FANNY STATS

09/27/2012
Date of Fanny's launch

26'10"
Fanny's height in feet and inches

51'6"
Fanny's length in feet and inches

12'
Fanny's body width in feet

39'
Fanny's wingspan in feet

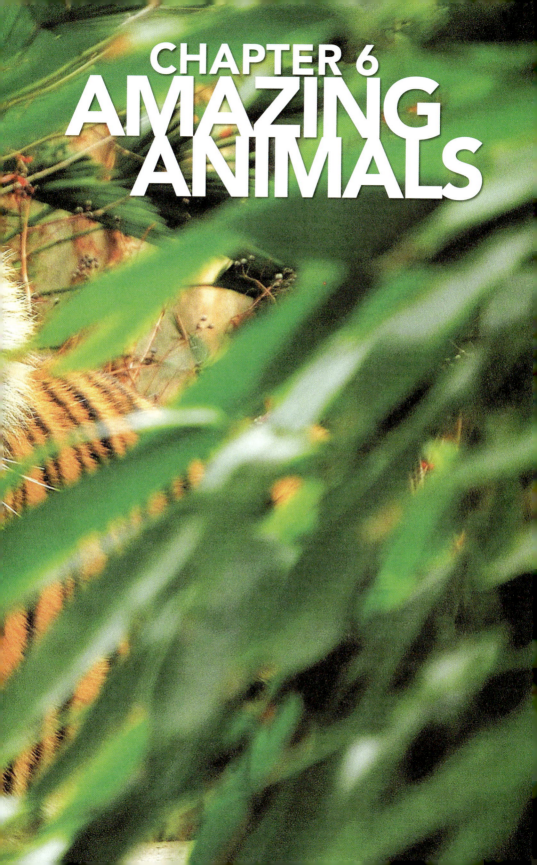

CHAPTER 6
AMAZING ANIMALS

AMAZING ANIMALS
trending

PRICEY ROCK **MOST EXPENSIVE FOSSIL** Standing at 11 feet tall and 20 feet long, "Apex" is considered the largest and most extensive *Stegosaurus* fossil ever found. The 150-million-year-old fossil made headlines when it was put up for auction at Sotheby's in May 2024. After frantic bidding that lasted fifteen minutes and involved seven interested parties from around the world, Apex was subject to a staggering and record-breaking bid of $44.6 million, becoming the most expensive fossil ever sold at auction.

WATERFRONT SPECTACLE **A SEA OF SEA LIONS IN SAN FRANCISCO** Sea lions are a common sight at San Francisco's Pier 39, but in May 2024, there were more of them than usual. Attracted by an unprecedented, large concentration of herring and anchovies in the nearby bay, around 1,000 sea lions took up residence by the pier—the largest such gathering in fifteen years.

SMART APE SELF-MEDICATING ORANGUTAN

In June 2022, a Sumatran orangutan did something that researchers had never seen before. Days after suffering a wound to his cheek, the orangutan known as Rakus was spotted picking and chewing the leaves of the akar kuning (a well-known medicinal plant) before applying it to his face. Rakus repeated the behavior the next day, and within days, the wound was fully healed.

SACRED SIGHTING RARE WHITE BISON

When a rare white bison calf was spotted crossing a road in Yellowstone National Park on June 4, 2024, it sparked a wave of interest. White buffalo are sacred to several Native American tribes, including the Sioux, Cherokee, Navajo, Lakota, and Dakota peoples. Several of the tribes prophesize about white buffalo calves being born at a time of great change. According to the prophecies, the appearance of a white bison can be seen as both a blessing and a warning.

PESTO THE PENGUIN OVERSIZED CHICK BECOMES AN ONLINE SENSATION

In January 2024, caretakers at Australia's Sea Life Melbourne Aquarium were delighted when a king penguin chick emerged from its shell. The chick, called Pesto, was the first king penguin born at the aquarium in two years. Pesto soon had a huge online following. By September 2024, he weighed in at a whopping 51.8 pounds (adult penguins usually weigh 31–37 pounds) and was towering over his parents.

World's sleepiest animal

KOALA

Australia's koala sleeps for up to twenty hours a day and still manages to look sleepy when awake. This is due to the koala's unbelievably monotonous diet. It feeds, mostly at night, on the aromatic leaves of eucalyptus trees. The leaves have little nutritional or caloric value, so the marsupial saves energy by snoozing. It jams its rear end into a fork in the branches of its favorite tree so that it does not fall out while asleep.

FLYING SQUIRREL

Flying squirrels are champion animal gliders. The Japanese giant flying squirrel has been scientifically recorded making flights over distances of up to 164 feet from tree to tree. These creatures have been estimated to make 656-foot flights when flying downhill. The squirrel remains aloft using a special flap of skin on either side of its body, which stretches between its wrist and ankle. Its fluffy tail acts as a stabilizer to keep it steady, and the squirrel changes direction by twisting its wrists and moving its limbs.

WORLD'S BEST GLIDERS
Distance in feet

Animal glider	Distance
Flying squirrel	656
Flying fish	655
Colugo, or flying lemur	230
Draco, or flying lizard	197
Flying squid	164

Feet: 70 140 210 280 350 420 490 560 630 700

World's heaviest land animal

AFRICAN BUSH ELEPHANT

The African bush elephant is the world's largest living land animal. The biggest known bush elephant stood 13.8 feet at the shoulder and had an estimated weight of 13.5 tons. The African bush elephant is also the animal with the largest outer ears. The outsize flappers help keep the animal cool on the open savanna. The Asian elephant has much smaller earflaps because it lives in the forest and is not exposed to the same high temperatures.

This little critter, the Kitti's hog-nosed bat, measures just 1.3 inches long, with a wingspan of 6.7 inches, and weighs 0.07–0.10 ounces. It's tied for first place as the world's smallest mammal with Savi's Etruscan shrew, which is longer at 2.1 inches but lighter at 0.04–0.06 ounces. The bat lives in west-central Thailand and southeast Myanmar, and the shrew is found in areas from the Mediterranean to Southeast Asia.

World's tiniest bat

KITTI'S HOG-NOSED BAT

World's largest primate

GORILLA

The largest living primates on Earth are eastern gorillas, and the biggest subspecies among them is the very rare mountain gorilla. The tallest known was an adult male silverback, named for the color of the fur on his back. He stood 6.4 feet tall, but he was an exception—silverbacks generally grow no bigger than 5.9 feet tall. Gorillas have long arms. The record holder had an arm span measuring 8.9 feet, while adult male humans have an average arm span of just 5.9 feet.

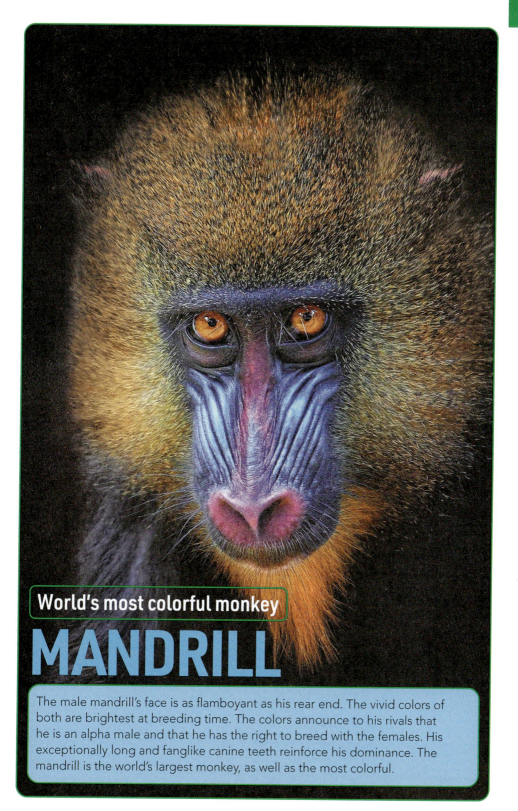

World's most colorful monkey

MANDRILL

The male mandrill's face is as flamboyant as his rear end. The vivid colors of both are brightest at breeding time. The colors announce to his rivals that he is an alpha male and that he has the right to breed with the females. His exceptionally long and fanglike canine teeth reinforce his dominance. The mandrill is the world's largest monkey, as well as the most colorful.

AMAZING ANIMALS

World's fastest land animal # CHEETAH

The fastest reliably recorded running speed of any animal was that of a zoo-bred cheetah that reached an incredible 61 miles per hour on a flat surface. The record was achieved in 2012 from a standing start by a captive cheetah at the Cincinnati Zoo. More recently, wild cheetahs have been timed while actually hunting their prey in the bush in Botswana. Using GPS technology and special tracking collars, the scientists found that these cheetahs had a top speed of 58 miles per hour over rough terrain.

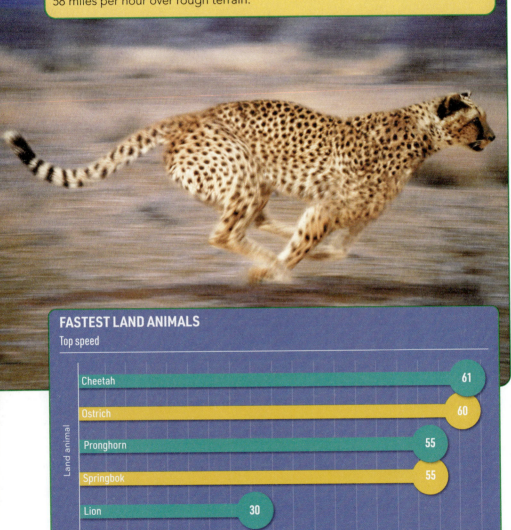

FASTEST LAND ANIMALS
Top speed

Land animal

Cheetah	61
Ostrich	60
Pronghorn	55
Springbok	55
Lion	30

6 12 18 24 30 36 42 48 54 60
mph

TIGER

There are only five big cats that roam Earth: the tiger, jaguar, leopard, lion, and snow leopard. The biggest and heaviest is the Siberian, or Amur, tiger, which lives in the taiga (boreal forest) of eastern Siberia, where it hunts deer and wild boar. The largest reliably measured tigers have been about 11.8 feet long and weighed around 705 pounds, but there have been claims of larger individuals, such as a male shot in the Sikhote-Alin Mountains in 1950. That tiger weighed 847 pounds.

World's tallest living animal

GIRAFFE

Giraffes living on the savannas of eastern and southern Africa are the world's tallest animals. The tallest known bull giraffe measured 19 feet from the ground to the top of his horns. He could have peered into the upstairs window of a two-story house. Despite having much longer necks than we do, giraffes have the same number of neck vertebrae. They also have long legs, with which they can either speedily escape from predators or kick them to keep them away.

GIRAFFE STATS

6 feet
Height of a calf at birth

25 years
Average lifespan

100 pounds
Adult's daily food consumption of leaves and twigs

World's noisiest land animal

HOWLER MONKEY

The howler monkeys of Central and South America are deafening. Males have an especially large hyoid bone. This horseshoe-shaped bone in the neck creates a chamber that makes the monkeys' deep guttural growls sound louder for longer. It is said that their calls can be heard up to 3 miles away. Both males and females call, and they holler mainly in the morning. It is thought that these calls are often one troop of monkeys telling neighboring troops where they are.

EPAULETTE SHARK

On Australia's Great Barrier Reef, and off the coasts of Indonesia and Papua New Guinea, lives a member of the carpet shark family that can walk! Called the epaulette shark, it is recognizable by a black spot, edged in white, on either side of its body. No more than 3 feet long, it lives in the intertidal zone, and when the tide goes out, it is often left stranded in a rock pool. As the temperature of the water rises in the heat, oxygen levels sink. But when oxygen levels get too low for the shark to survive, it uses its paddle-shaped pectoral fins to pull itself over the rocks from one pool to the next, until it finds one with more oxygen in the water.

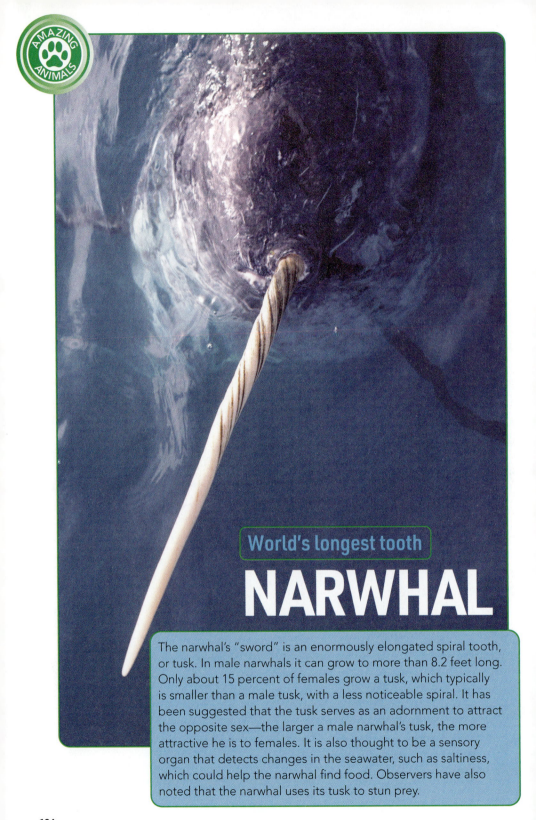

World's longest tooth

NARWHAL

The narwhal's "sword" is an enormously elongated spiral tooth, or tusk. In male narwhals it can grow to more than 8.2 feet long. Only about 15 percent of females grow a tusk, which typically is smaller than a male tusk, with a less noticeable spiral. It has been suggested that the tusk serves as an adornment to attract the opposite sex—the larger a male narwhal's tusk, the more attractive he is to females. It is also thought to be a sensory organ that detects changes in the seawater, such as saltiness, which could help the narwhal find food. Observers have also noted that the narwhal uses its tusk to stun prey.

World's largest living animal

BLUE WHALE

Blue whales are truly colossal. The largest one accurately measured was 110 feet long, and the heaviest weighed 209 tons. They feed on tiny krill, which they filter from the sea. The largest known animal on land was a titanosaur—a huge dinosaur that lived 101 million years ago in what is now Argentina. A skeleton found in 2014 suggests the creature was 121 feet long and weighed 77 tons. It belonged to a young titanosaur, so an adult may have been bigger than a blue whale.

World's biggest fish

WHALE SHARK

Recognizable from its spotted skin and enormous size, the whale shark is the world's largest living fish. It grows to a maximum length of about 66 feet. Like the blue whale, this fish feeds on some of the smallest creatures: krill, marine larvae, small fish, and fish eggs. The whale shark is also a great traveler. One female was tracked swimming 4,800 miles from Mexico—where hundreds of whale sharks gather each summer to feed—to the middle of the South Atlantic Ocean, where it is thought she may have given birth.

GREAT WHITE SHARK

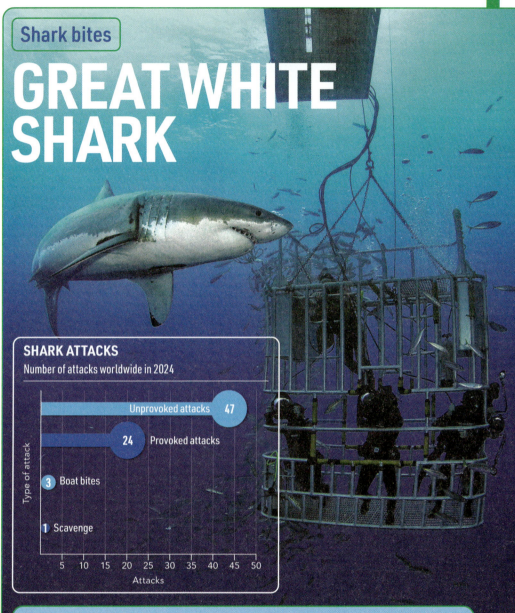

SHARK ATTACKS

Number of attacks worldwide in 2024

Type of attack

Unprovoked attacks	47
24	Provoked attacks
3	Boat bites
1	Scavenge

5 10 15 20 25 30 35 40 45 50

Attacks

The great white shark is considered the animal most likely to make an unprovoked attack on people. Of the 949 shark attacks recorded over the last 400 years, 351 have been attributed to great whites—fifty-nine of them fatal. The biggest reliably measured great white was 21 feet long, making it the largest predatory fish in the sea. Its jaws are lined with 3-inch-long, triangular, serrated teeth that can slice through flesh, sinew, and even bone. Of the forty-seven unprovoked shark attacks in 2024, only four were fatal. Humans are not a shark's food of choice; they don't have enough fat on their bodies. White sharks, in particular, prefer blubber-rich seals and dolphins. It is likely that many of the attacks on people are probably cases of mistaken identity.

World's largest lizard

KOMODO DRAGON

There are dragons on Indonesia's Komodo Island, and they're dangerous. The Komodo dragon's jaws are lined with sixty replaceable, serrated, backward-pointing teeth. Its saliva is laced with deadly bacteria and venom that the dragon works into a wound, ensuring its prey will die quickly. Because this is the world's largest lizard, prey can be as big as a pig or a deer. It can grow up to 10.3 feet long and weigh 366 pounds.

POISON DART FROG

A poison dart frog's skin exudes toxins. There are several species, and the more vivid a frog's color, the more deadly its poison. The skin color warns potential predators that the frogs are not good to eat, although one animal—the fire-bellied snake—is immune to the chemicals and happily feeds on these creatures. It is thought that the frogs do not manufacture their own poisons, but obtain the chemicals from their diet of ants, millipedes, and mites. The most deadly species to humans is also the largest poison dart frog: Colombia's golden poison dart frog. At just 1 inch long, a single frog has enough poison to kill ten to twenty people.

World's largest reptile

SALTWATER CROCODILE

The saltwater crocodile, or "saltie," is the world's largest living reptile. Males can grow to over 20 feet long, but a few old-timers become real monsters. A well-known crocodile in the Segama River, Borneo, Malaysia, left an impression on a sandbank that measured 33 feet. The saltie can be found in areas from eastern India to northeastern Australia, where it lives in mangroves, estuaries, and rivers. It is sometimes found out at sea. The saltie is an ambush predator, grabbing any animal that enters its domain—including humans. Saltwater crocodiles account for twenty to thirty attacks on people per year, up to half of which are fatal.

NANO-CHAMELEON

In a mountain forest in northern Madagascar lives the smallest known reptile in the world: the nano-chameleon *Brookesia nana*. From his snout to the tip of his tail, the male of the species is just 0.85 inches long—roughly the length of a sunflower seed. The female is a little longer: 1.14 inches. They live among the leaf litter on the forest floor, where they hunt for mites and springtails. They are well camouflaged with a light-brown-and-gray body, and they hide from predators among blades of grass. Unlike most chameleons, they do not change color, but they do have the chameleon's long, extendable tongue to capture prey.

131

HOATZIN

The hoatzin eats leaves, flowers, and fruit. It ferments the food in its crop (a pouch in its esophagus). This habit leaves the bird with a foul odor, which has led people to nickname the hoatzin the "stinkbird." About the size of a pheasant, this bird lives in the Amazon and Orinoco river basins of South America. A hoatzin chick has sharp claws on its wings, like a pterodactyl. If threatened by a snake, the chick jumps from the nest into the water, using its wing claws to help it climb back up.

AMAZING ANIMALS

The ribbon-tailed astrapia has the longest feathers in relation to body size of any wild bird. The male, which has a beautiful, iridescent blue-green head, sports a pair of white ribbon-shaped tail feathers that are more than 3.3 feet long—three times the length of its 13-inch-long body. It is one of Papua New Guinea's birds of paradise and lives in the mountain forests of central New Guinea, where males sometimes have to untangle their tails from the foliage before they can fly.

Bird with the longest tail

RIBBON-TAILED ASTRAPIA

Bird that builds the largest nest

BALD EAGLE

With a wingspan of more than 6.6 feet, bald eagles need space to land and take off—so their nests can be gargantuan. Over the years, a nest built by a pair of bald eagles in St. Petersburg, Florida, has taken on epic proportions. Measuring 9.5 feet across and 20 feet deep, it is made of sticks, grass, and moss. At one stage, it was thought to have weighed at least 2 tons, making it the largest nest ever constructed by a pair of birds. Although one pair nests at a time, these huge structures are often the work of several pairs of birds, each building on top of the work of their predecessors.

World's largest bird egg

AFRICAN OSTRICH EGG

The African ostrich lays the largest eggs of any living bird, yet they are the smallest eggs relative to the size of the mother's body. Each egg is some 5.9 inches long and weighs about 3.5–5 pounds, while the mother is about 6.2 feet tall and the father is about 7.8 feet tall, making the ostrich the world's largest living bird. The female lays about fifty eggs per year, and each egg contains as much yolk and albumen as twenty-four hens' eggs. It takes an hour to soft-boil an ostrich egg!

World's biggest penguin

EMPEROR PENGUIN

At 4 feet tall, the emperor penguin is the world's biggest living penguin. It has a most curious lifestyle, breeding during the long, dark Antarctic winter. The female lays a single egg and carefully passes it to the male. She then heads out to sea to feed, while he remains with the egg balanced on his feet and tucked under a fold of blubber-rich skin. There he stands with all the other penguin dads, huddled together to keep warm in the blizzards and 100-mile-per-hour winds that scour the icy continent. Come spring, the egg hatches, the female returns, and Mom and Dad swap duties, taking turns feeding and caring for their fluffy chick.

EMPEROR PENGUIN STATS

80 pounds
Average weight of an adult

1,751 feet
Depth to which an adult can swim

22 minutes
Length of time an adult can stay underwater

FIVE OF THE WORLD'S BIGGEST PENGUINS
Height in inches

- Emperor
- King
- Gentoo
- Macaroni
- Galápagos

Inches

Emperor	48
King	39
Gentoo	35
Macaroni	28
Galápagos	19

World's heaviest spider

GOLIATH BIRD-EATING
TARANTULA

The size of a dinner plate, the female goliath bird-eating tarantula has a leg span of 11 inches and weighs up to 6.17 ounces. This is the world's heaviest spider and a real nightmare for an arachnophobe (someone with a fear of spiders). Its fangs can pierce a person's skin, but its venom is no worse than a bee sting. The hairs on its body are more of a hazard. When threatened, it rubs its abdomen with its hind legs and releases tiny hairs that can cause severe irritation to the skin. Despite its name, this spider does not actually eat birds very often.

World's biggest hornet ASIAN
GIANT HORNET

At 2 inches long, with a 0.25-inch stinger and fearsome jaws, the Asian giant hornet is more than twice the size of other hornet species. While native to Asia, this hornet is also known in the Pacific Northwest. Preying on honeybees, a swarm of giant hornets can wipe out an entire hive in only a couple of hours. This is a problem for farmers, whose crops need honeybees to pollinate them. In the Pacific Northwest, for example, honeybees are crucial to the successful harvest of cherries, apples, and blueberries. Thankfully, the hornet nests are a rare sight in the United States and farmers are developing ways to protect their bees.

World's fastest known animal movement in nature

DRACULA ANT

The Dracula ant, *Mystrium camillae*, of tropical areas of Africa, Southeast Asia, and Australasia, makes the fastest movement of any known animal on Earth. In the time it takes you to blink, it can open and close its jaws *five thousand* times. It does this by pressing its jaws together, storing energy like a spring, and then sliding them past each other at up to 200 miles per hour. Such fast jaws allow the ant to stun or kill its prey, such as fast-moving centipedes, which have their own formidable jaws!

World's fastest flying insect

DESERT LOCUST

Flying insects are difficult to clock, and many impressive speeds have been claimed over the years. The fastest airspeed reliably timed was by fifteen desert locusts that managed an average of 21 miles per hour. Airspeed is the actual speed at which the insect flies. It is different from ground speed, which is often enhanced by favorable winds. A black cutworm moth whizzed along at 70 miles per hour while riding the winds ahead of a cold front. The most shocking measurement, however, is that of a horsefly with an estimated airspeed of 90 miles per hour while chasing an air-gun pellet! Understandably, this is one speed that has not been verified!

World's deadliest animal

MOSQUITO

Female mosquitoes live on the blood of birds and mammals—humans included. However, the problem is not what they take, but what they leave behind. In some mosquitoes' saliva are organisms that cause the world's most deadly illnesses, including malaria, yellow fever, dengue fever, West Nile virus, and encephalitis. It is estimated that mosquitoes transmit diseases to 700 million people every year, of which 725,000 die. In 2021, the World Health Organization (WHO) announced the release of a vaccine that can help prevent a mosquito-borne disease called malaria, and that has the potential to save tens of thousands of lives.

GLOBE SKIMMER

Each year, millions of dragonflies fly thousands of miles across the Indian Ocean from South India to East Africa. Most of them are globe skimmers, a species known to fly long distances and at altitudes up to 3,280 feet. They can travel 2,175 miles in 24 hours. Coral cays on the way have little open fresh water, so the insects stay there for a few days before moving on to East Africa. There, they follow the rains, at each stop taking advantage of temporary rainwater pools to lay their eggs to hatch where their young can rapidly develop. Four generations are involved in a round trip of about 11,000 miles—farther than the distance from New York City to Sydney.

trending

CLEVER KITTY
THE LONG WAY HOME

On June 4, 2024, Susanne and Benny Anguiano's cat Rayne Beau disappeared at a Yellowstone National Park campsite. They searched for five days before having to give up and return home to California. Remarkably, by July 31, Rayne Beau had made the 800-mile journey all the way to Roseville, California—about 200 miles from his family home. Thanks to a microchip, he was soon reunited with his astonished owners.

CANINE CAPERS SUPERSMART DOGS

Bonnie and Simba, trained by Olga Jones, might be the world's smartest dogs. The English canine duo hold a number of world records, for fastest time to complete ten leapfrog jumps by two dogs (16.78 seconds); most clothes hung on a washing line by a dog in one minute (17); most bottles deposited in a bin by a dog in one minute (16); and most coins deposited into a bottle by a dog in one minute (13).

WOOF, WOOF DOG-FRIENDLY AIRLINE

It was not the world's first, but in May 2024 a new, dog-friendly airline, Bark Air, was launched. It puts dogs and their owners first. Before takeoff, dogs snack on treats and wear noise-canceling earmuffs to help them relax. The dogs remain with their owners during the flight. The experience does not come cheap, however. A single ticket from New York to Los Angeles for a dog and owner costs $6,000.

ATTABOY! KOBE THE LIFESAVING DOG

When pet dog Kobe started digging a hole in the backyard, his owner, Chanell Bell, knew something was up. Her house had recently suffered a gas leak, so she decided to check gas levels in the hole. It was lucky she did! Her husky had discovered a major gas leak that could have had a devastating effect on the entire neighborhood.

NEW CHAMPION? FRED THE GIANT DONKEY

With the passing of America's huge donkey Romulus in 2024, there could be a new contender for world's tallest donkey. Fred is a ten-year-old who lives on Katharina Perutzki's Kuschelfarm sanctuary in Saxony, Germany. When Romulus entered the *Guinness Book of Records* in 2013, he measured 5 feet, 8 inches tall. German Fred is half an inch taller! Perutzki is hoping he will be accepted as the next Guinness Record holder.

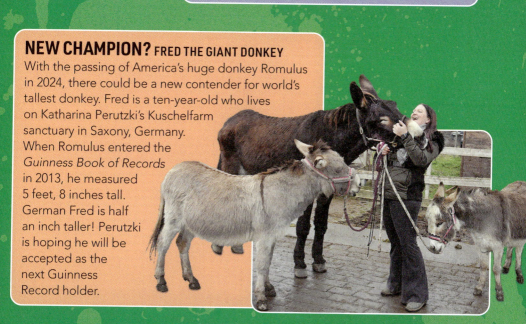

145

World's fluffiest rabbit

ANGORA RABBIT

In most people's opinion, the Angora rabbit is the world's fluffiest bunny. The breed originated in Turkey and is thought to be one of the world's oldest rabbit breeds as well. It became popular with the French court in the mid-eighteenth century. Today, it is bred for its long, soft wool, which is shorn every three to four months. One of the fluffiest bunnies ever was buff-colored Franchesca, owned by English Angora rabbit expert Dr. Betty Chu. In 2014, Franchesca's fur was measured at 14.37 inches, a world record that has yet to be beaten.

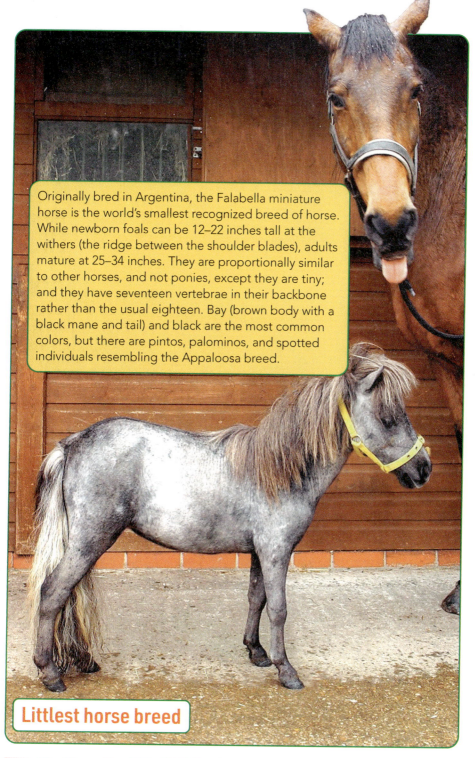

Originally bred in Argentina, the Falabella miniature horse is the world's smallest recognized breed of horse. While newborn foals can be 12–22 inches tall at the withers (the ridge between the shoulder blades), adults mature at 25–34 inches. They are proportionally similar to other horses, and not ponies, except they are tiny; and they have seventeen vertebrae in their backbone rather than the usual eighteen. Bay (brown body with a black mane and tail) and black are the most common colors, but there are pintos, palominos, and spotted individuals resembling the Appaloosa breed.

Littlest horse breed

FALABELLA

World's hairiest dog

KOMONDOR

The world's hairiest dog breed is the Komondor, or Hungarian sheepdog. It is a powerful dog that was bred originally to guard sheep. Its long, white, dreadlock-like "cords" enable it to not only blend in with the flock but also protect itself from bad weather and bites from wolves. This is a large dog, standing over 27.5 inches at the shoulders. Its hairs are up to 10.6 inches long, giving it the heaviest coat of any dog.

FRENCH BULLDOG

According to the American Kennel Club, the French Bulldog remained the club's favorite dog breed for the third year running in 2024. Known affectionately as the "Frenchie," this cute, playful little dog is a bulldog in miniature, right down to the wrinkled face, snub nose, and "bat" ears. In 2022, the Frenchie brought an end to the Labrador Retriever's reign as the country's no. 1 breed, which lasted an incredible thirty-one years. It looks as if the adorable little bulldog is here to stay!

AMERICA'S MOST POPULAR DOGS, 2024

1. French Bulldog
2. Labrador Retriever
3. Golden Retriever
4. German Shepherd Dog
5. Poodle
6. Dachshund
7. Beagle
8. Rottweiler
9. Bulldog
10. German Shorthaired Pointer

World's longest-lived land animal

JONATHAN

Having celebrated his 190th birthday in 2022, Jonathan the tortoise is believed to be the world's longest-lived land animal. He hatched around 1832 on the Aldabra Atoll, part of the Seychelles archipelago in the Indian Ocean. Since 1882, he's been living on a distant island in another ocean—St. Helena, part of a British overseas territory in the South Atlantic—where he was presented to the governor at the time as a gift. Today, he lives on the lawn in front of Plantation House, the official residence of the governor of St. Helena, with three other giant tortoises. Jonathan puts his longevity down to a healthy diet of fresh grass and fruit.

The Chihuahua is the world's smallest dog breed. Originating in the northern Mexican state of Chihuahua, it is probably a descendant of the Techichi, a mute companion dog of the Toltec civilization, dating back to the ninth century CE. The breed today averages 5–8 inches tall and weighs 3–6 pounds, although the world's smallest dog ever, a Chihuahua by the name of Miracle Milly, was just 3.8 inches tall and weighed no more than a pound, not much bigger than a sneaker.

World's smallest dog breed

CHIHUAHUA

World's most popular cat breed

MAINE COON CAT

AMERICA'S MOST POPULAR CATS, 2025

1. Maine Coon Cat
2. Ragdoll
3. Persian
4. Exotic
5. Devon Rex
6. Abyssinian
7. British Shorthair
8. Siberian
9. Sphynx
10. Russian Blue

In March 2025, the Cat Fanciers' Association announced that the Maine Coon Cat was the world's most popular cat breed. A real gentle giant, Maine Coon Cats are sociable, intelligent, and playful. Their regal good looks and charm have made them this year's top cat. This is the first year that this big cat has taken the top spot as the most registered cat breed of the previous year. The year's listings also saw the Ragdoll play second fiddle and the Russian Blue enter the list, knocking the Scottish Fold out of the top 10.

World's baldest cat

SPHYNX

The Sphynx breed of cats is famous for its wrinkles and the lack of a normal coat, but it is not entirely hairless. Its skin is like the softest chamois leather, but it has a thin layer of down. It behaves more like a dog than a cat, greets its owners when they come home, and is friendly to strangers. The breed originated in Canada, where a black-and-white cat gave birth to a hairless kitten called Prune in 1966. Subsequent breeding gave rise to the Sphynx.

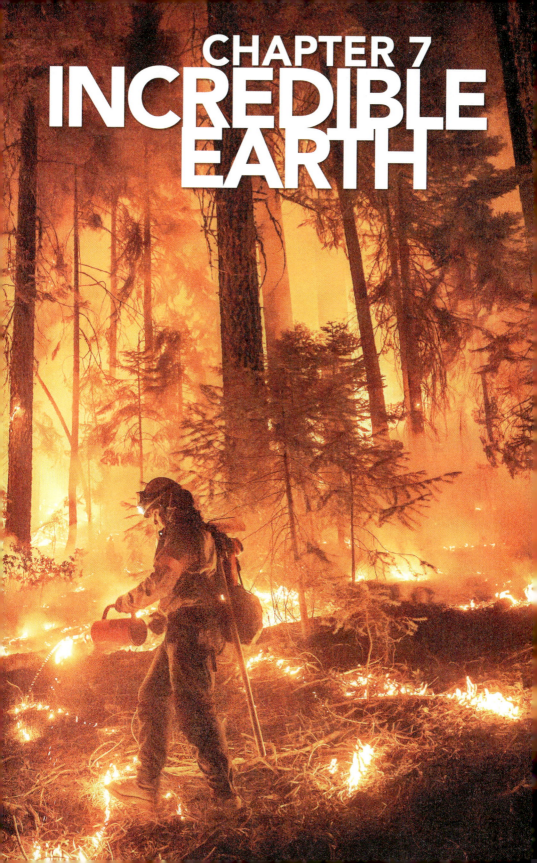

CHAPTER 7
INCREDIBLE EARTH

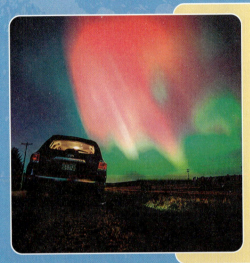

MAGNETIC STORM NORTHERN LIGHTS OVER THE SOUTH! In October 2024, a severe solar storm made the aurora borealis—also known as the northern lights—visible as far south in the United States as Texas, Arizona, and Mississippi—way farther south than normal. It was caused by a fast-moving coronal mass ejection, a powerful burst of magnetized plasma from the sun's corona, which had the effect of increasing the energy to Earth's magnetic field. Although this might sound like a dramatic event, it had little effect on everyday life.

RARE EVENT SOLAR ECLIPSE ACROSS AMERICA
On April 8, 2024, millions of Americans watched as the moon passed in front of the sun, plunging swaths of the United States into temporary darkness. According to NASA, an estimated 31.6 million Americans lived in the path of a total solar eclipse, with another 150 million people living within 200 miles of it. The next solar eclipse visible from the contiguous United States will take place on August 24, 2044.

MEGA ROCK BIG DIAMOND The Karowe diamond mine, 300 miles north of Botswana's capital Gaborone, is famous for producing exceptionally large diamonds. In the last decade, miners have unearthed some gigantic stones, but in August 2024, the mine produced its biggest yet: an enormous 2,492-carat diamond—the second-largest diamond ever discovered and the largest since the 3,106-carat Cullinan diamond was discovered in South Africa in 1905.

GETTING WARMER HOTTEST SUMMER FOR 2,000 YEARS Global temperatures have been increasing due to human activity that releases greenhouse gases into the atmosphere. By analyzing tree-ring data (tree rings grow wider in warmer temperatures) to compare temperatures as far back as 1 CE, scientists have discovered that last summer was the hottest summer in the northern hemisphere in the last 2,000 years.

ANCIENT EARTH HOW DID THE WORLD LOOK MILLIONS OF YEARS AGO? Have you ever wanted to see how much a specific location has changed over the past 750 million years? Well, an interactive tool called Ancient Earth allows you to do just that. The brainchild of Ian Webster, who is the curator of the world's largest digital dinosaur database, this tool allows you to type in a location and then choose a date ranging from zero to 750 million years ago.

Oldest tree on Earth

BRISTLECONE PINE

An unnamed bristlecone pine in the White Mountains of California is the world's oldest continuously standing tree. It is 5,074 years old, beating its bristlecone rival, the Methuselah (4,856 years old), by 218 years. Although Methuselah officially holds the record for the oldest-living tree, Alerce Milenario, also known as Gran Abuelo (great-grandfather), is also a contender. A Chilean scientist working in Paris claims the alerce tree is more than 5,000 years old, which would beat the existing record holder, but not everyone agrees with the scientist's assessment. He used computer models to calculate the tree's age, based on just a partial section of its trunk—so he hasn't counted all the tree rings.

World's tallest tree

CALIFORNIA REDWOOD

WORLD'S TALLEST TREES
Height in feet

- Coast redwood, California, US
- Mountain ash, Styx Valley, Tasmania
- Coast Douglas-fir, Oregon, US
- Sitka spruce, California, US
- Giant sequoia, California, US

Tree	Height (feet)
Coast redwood	379.1
Mountain ash	327.4
Coast Douglas-fir	327.3
Sitka spruce	317.0
Giant sequoia	314.0

A coast redwood named Hyperion is the world's tallest known living tree. It is 379.1 feet tall, and could have grown taller if a woodpecker had not hammered its top. It's growing in a remote part of the Redwood National and State Parks in Northern California, but its exact location is kept a secret for fear that too many visitors would upset its ecosystem. It is thought to be 700–800 years old.

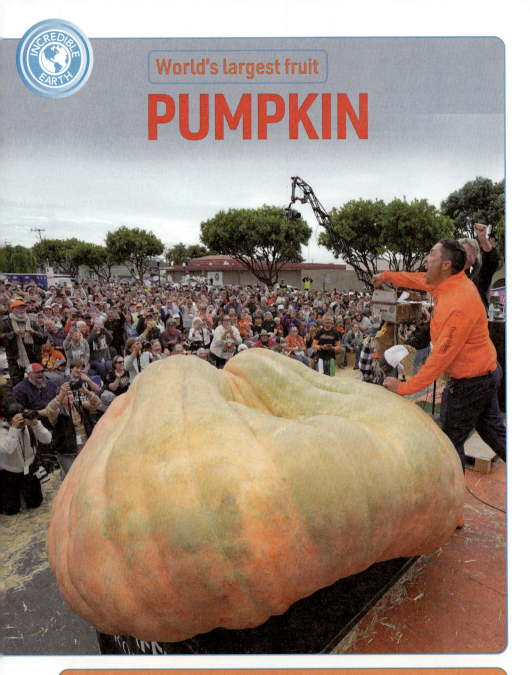

World's largest fruit
PUMPKIN

Pumpkins are known for being large fruits, but with a bit of horticultural nudging, they can grow to be truly monstrous. Gourd-grower Travis Gienger's colossal triumph proved this point at the 2023 World Championship Pumpkin Weigh-Off held in Half Moon Bay, California. Weighing in at a record-breaking 2,749 pounds, the pumpkin was heavier than a small family car. Grown from a 2365 Wolf seed (a new type known for yielding especially large pumpkins), and dubbed "Michael Jordan" due to its resemblance to a basketball, the pumpkin was big enough to make more than 650 pies.

The leaf of the giant Amazon water lily can grow as wide as 8.6 feet across. It has an upturned rim and a waxy, water-repellent upper surface. On the underside of the leaf is a riblike structure that traps air, enabling the leaf to float easily. The ribs are also lined with sharp spines that protect them from aquatic plant eaters. A full-grown leaf is so large and so strong that it can support up to 99 pounds in weight.

GIANT AMAZON WATER LILY

World's largest cave

HANG SON DOONG
VIETNAM

Measuring 1.35 billion cubic feet, Hang Son Doong, in Vietnam, is the world's largest cave by volume. It was first discovered in 1991 by an elderly man collecting firewood, and he later revealed its location to a British caving expedition. When the explorers lit up the cave with their powerful lamps, they discovered caverns of immense size. In one, a jumbo jet could sit comfortably on the floor, with room to spare, and you could fit in a tall skyscraper, too. The explorers went on to discover the world's tallest stalagmites—up to 250 feet tall—and a 300-foot-high calcite wall, which they nicknamed the "Great Wall of Vietnam."

GARDEN OF EDAM

At two points in the vast cave system, explorers found that the roof had collapsed and light spilled in, forming a huge circular hole, or doline. The largest of the two dolines, the Garden of Edam, features a tropical rainforest in the center of the cave, with some trees 100 feet tall and inhabitants that include lizards, birds, and monkeys.

HANG SON DOONG

Mountain river cave
Name's meaning

1991
Year of discovery

5.6 miles
Total length

1.35 billion cubic feet
Total volume of the world's largest cave

Deepest point on land

DENMAN GLACIER

The deepest point on land has been discovered under the Denman Glacier in East Antarctica. Deep below the Antarctic ice sheet, which is 1.3 miles thick on average, there is an ice-filled canyon whose floor is 11,500 feet below sea level. By comparison, the lowest clearly visible point on land is in the Jordan Rift Valley, on the shore of the Dead Sea, just 1,412 feet below sea level. It makes the Denman canyon the deepest canyon on land. Only trenches at the bottom of the ocean are deeper. The floor of the deepest trench—the Mariana Trench—is close to 7 miles below the sea's surface.

GEYSER FIELDS

Number of geysers

- Yellowstone, Idaho/Montana/ Wyoming, US
- Valley of Geysers, Kamchatka, Russia
- El Tatio, Andes, Chile
- Orakei Korako, New Zealand
- Hveravellir, Iceland

Number of geysers

600
540
480
420
360
300
240
180
120
60

540

139

84

33

16

World's greatest number of geysers

YELLOWSTONE NATIONAL PARK

There are about 1,000 geysers that erupt worldwide, and 540 of them are in Yellowstone National Park, US. That's the greatest concentration of geysers on Earth. The most famous is Old Faithful, which spews out a cloud of steam and hot water to a maximum height of 185 feet every 44 to 125 minutes. Yellowstone's spectacular water display is due to its closeness to molten rock from Earth's mantle that rises up to the surface. One day the park could face an eruption 1,000 times as powerful as that of Mount St. Helens in 1980.

MOUNT EVEREST

Mount Everest has grown. In December 2020, Nepal and China agreed on an official height that is 2.8 feet higher than the previous calculation. The mega mountain is located in the Himalayan mountain range, on the border between Tibet and Nepal. The mountain acquired its official name from surveyor Sir George Everest, but local people know it as Chomolungma (Tibet) or Sagarmatha (Nepal). In 1953, Sir Edmund Hillary and Tenzing Norgay were the first people to reach its summit. Now more than 650 people per year manage to make the spectacular climb.

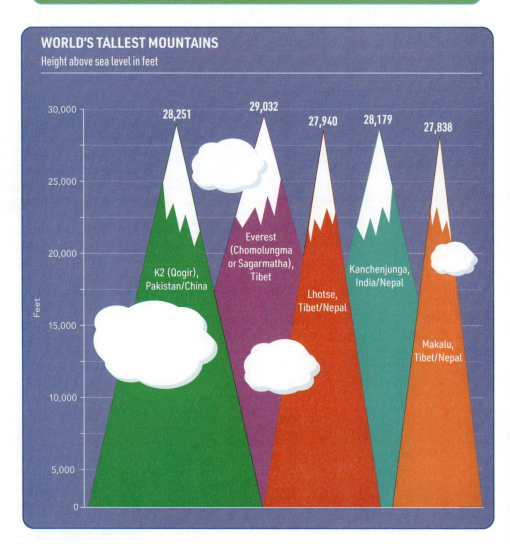

WORLD'S TALLEST MOUNTAINS
Height above sea level in feet

28,251 — K2 (Qogir), Pakistan/China
29,032 — Everest (Chomolungma or Sagarmatha), Tibet
27,940 — Lhotse, Tibet/Nepal
28,179 — Kanchenjunga, India/Nepal
27,838 — Makalu, Tibet/Nepal

GREAT BARRIER REEF

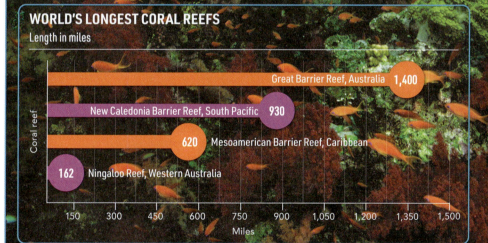

WORLD'S LONGEST CORAL REEFS

Length in miles

Coral reef

- Great Barrier Reef, Australia **1,400**
- New Caledonia Barrier Reef, South Pacific **930**
- **620** Mesoamerican Barrier Reef, Caribbean
- **162** Ningaloo Reef, Western Australia

150 300 450 600 750 900 1,050 1,200 1,350 1,500

Miles

Australia's Great Barrier Reef is the only living thing that's clearly visible from space. It stretches along the Queensland coast for 1,400 miles, making it the longest coral reef system in the world. At its northern tip, scientists have discovered a towering, blade-shaped reef, taller than the Empire State Building, that is a mile wide at its base and tapers to a knife edge about 130 feet below the surface. In recent years, climate change has posed a huge threat to the world's coral reefs, with rising sea temperatures causing areas to die off. The northern half of the Great Barrier Reef suffered particularly in 2016, and scientists fear that more damage is yet to come.

167

World's largest hot desert

SAHARA DESERT

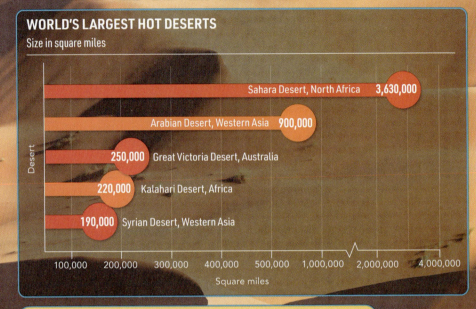

WORLD'S LARGEST HOT DESERTS

Size in square miles

Desert

Sahara Desert, North Africa — **3,630,000**

Arabian Desert, Western Asia — **900,000**

250,000 Great Victoria Desert, Australia

220,000 Kalahari Desert, Africa

190,000 Syrian Desert, Western Asia

100,000 200,000 300,000 400,000 500,000 1,000,000 2,000,000 4,000,000

Square miles

Sahara means simply "great desert," and great it is. It's the largest hot desert on the planet. It's almost the same size as the United States or China and dominates North Africa from the Atlantic Ocean in the west to the Red Sea in the east. This desert is extremely dry, with most of the Sahara receiving less than 0.1 inch of rain a year, and some places getting none at all for several years. It is stiflingly hot, up to 122°F, making this one of the hottest and driest regions in the world.

CASPIAN SEA

The countries of Russia, Kazakhstan, Turkmenistan, Iran, and Azerbaijan border the vast Caspian Sea, the largest inland body of water on Earth. Once part of an ancient sea, the lake became landlocked between five and ten million years ago, with occasional fills of salt water as sea levels fluctuated over time. Now it has a surface area of about 149,200 square miles and is home to one of the world's most valuable fish: the beluga sturgeon, the source of beluga caviar, which costs up to $2,250 per pound.

WORLD'S LARGEST LAKES

Area in square miles

Lake	Area
Caspian Sea, Europe/Asia	149,200
Lake Superior, North America	31,700
Lake Victoria, Africa	26,828
Lake Huron, North America	23,000
Lake Michigan, North America	22,300

30,000   60,000   90,000   120,000   150,000

Square miles

World's longest river

NILE RIVER

Flowing from south to north through eastern Africa, the Nile River is the world's longest. It begins in rivers that flow into Lake Victoria, which borders modern-day Uganda, Tanzania, and Kenya. One of those rivers is the Kagera River. From the lake, the Nile proper heads north across eastern Africa for 4,132 miles to the Mediterranean. Its water is crucial to people living along its banks. They use it to irrigate precious crops, generate electricity, and, in the lower reaches, as a river highway.

WORLD'S LONGEST RIVERS
Length in miles

River	Miles
Nile River, Africa	4,132
Amazon River, South America	4,000
Yangtze River, China	3,915
Mississippi–Missouri river system, US	3,710
Yellow River, China	3,395

Miles: 1,000 · 2,000 · 3,000 · 4,000

NAZARÉ

The town of Nazaré in Portugal is famous for the mountainous surf that makes landfall there. German-born and Hawaii-trained Sebastian Steudtner rode the highest wave ever recorded there. Aided by the seafloor topography and the direction of the wind, the wave rose to a massive 86 feet, enabling Steudtner to claim the world record for surfing the "largest wave." He achieved a near-perfect ride, staying ahead of the curling wave immediately behind him and exiting gently to one side before the gigantic wall of water came crashing down. However, on December 23, 2024, surfer Alo Slebir rode a wave that is estimated to be 108 feet high, putting Steudtner's record in jeopardy.

WILDFIRES 2024-2025

In 2024 and early 2025, it often felt as if the whole planet was on fire. Wildfires consumed great swaths of South America, Russia, central Africa, Southeast Asia, Australia and New Zealand, Canada, the western United States, and several Mediterranean nations.

UNITED STATES

California started 2025 with wind-driven fires that destroyed thousands of Los Angeles homes, several historic landmarks, and two urban commercial districts. The previous year, much of rural Northern California was devastated by wildfires that burned through a state record 1.9 million acres after years of drought and warm weather. In Oregon, the forest fires of 2024 were so ferocious they created their own weather, with thunder and lightning that ignited even more blazes.

CANADA

A blaze caused by an electrical storm threatened Jasper, Canada. Fires started in the mountains on either side of the resort town and converged to form a 328-foot-high firewall that swept through it. Cars melted, forming pools of molten metal. Officials ordered a mass evacuation of 25,000 people, and many lost their properties, although several key buildings, such as the hospital and schools, were unscathed.

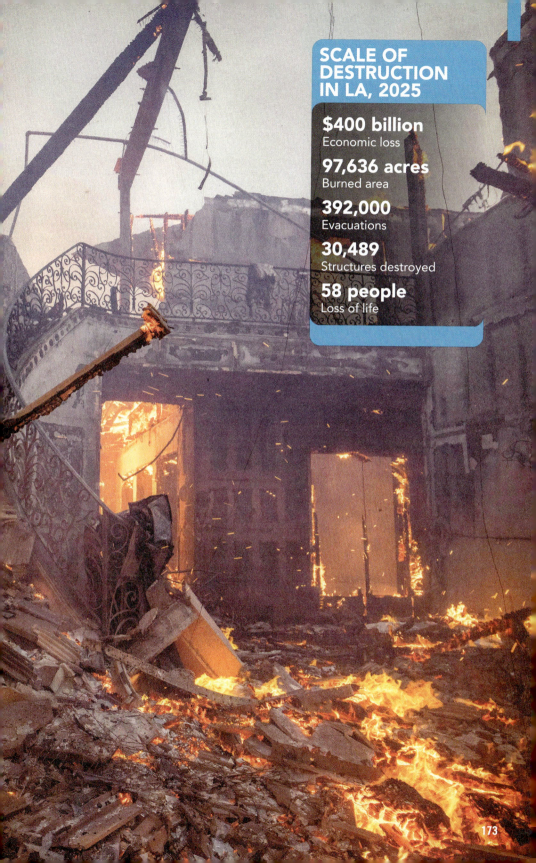

SCALE OF DESTRUCTION IN LA, 2025

$400 billion
Economic loss

97,636 acres
Burned area

392,000
Evacuations

30,489
Structures destroyed

58 people
Loss of life

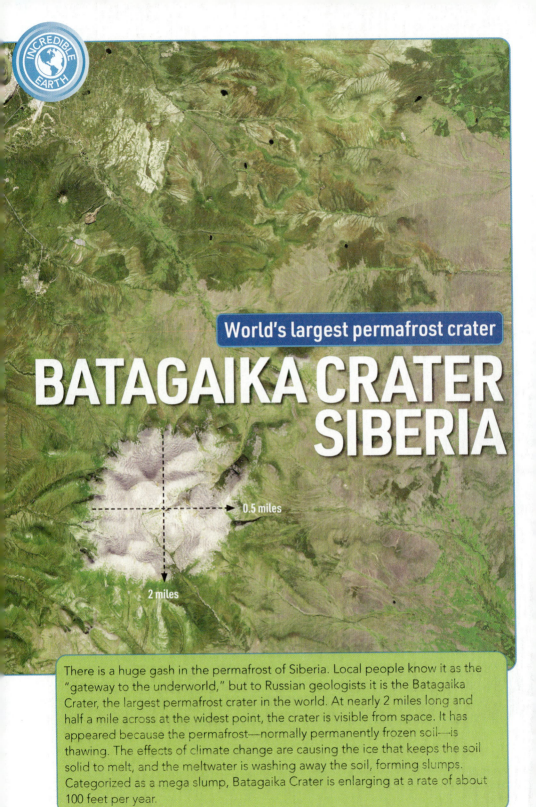

World's largest permafrost crater

BATAGAIKA CRATER SIBERIA

0.5 miles

2 miles

There is a huge gash in the permafrost of Siberia. Local people know it as the "gateway to the underworld," but to Russian geologists it is the Batagaika Crater, the largest permafrost crater in the world. At nearly 2 miles long and half a mile across at the widest point, the crater is visible from space. It has appeared because the permafrost—normally permanently frozen soil—is thawing. The effects of climate change are causing the ice that keeps the soil solid to melt, and the meltwater is washing away the soil, forming slumps. Categorized as a mega slump, Batagaika Crater is enlarging at a rate of about 100 feet per year.

Longest lightning flash

UNITED STATES

In February 2022, the World Meteorological Organization (WMO) announced a new record for the world's longest single lightning flash, which it had discovered by scanning satellite imagery. The strike occurred two years earlier, on April 29, 2020. In the event, a 477.2-mile-long megaflash of lightning ripped through the skies above Mississippi, Louisiana, and Texas—quite a record, given that strikes rarely stretch over 10 miles. The megaflash was just 36 miles longer than the previous record holder, a 440.6-mile-long strike in Brazil on October 31, 2018.

Hottest month ever

JULY 2024

The National Oceanic and Atmospheric Administration declared July 2024 to be the hottest month on record globally, 0.05°F higher than in July 2023, and the highest since 1850. The extreme weather led the Secretary-General of the United Nations to state that "Earth is becoming hotter and more dangerous for everyone, everywhere," and for the Secretary-General of the World Meteorological Organization to indicate that "widespread, intense, and extended heat waves have hit every continent in the past year. At least ten countries have recorded daily temperatures of more than [122°F] in more than one location. This is becoming too hot to handle."

CALIFORNIA AND COLORADO

The greatest depth of snow on record in the United States occurred at Tamarack, near the Bear Valley ski resort in California, on March 11, 1911. The snow reached an incredible 37.8 feet deep. Tamarack also holds the record for the most snowfall in a single month, with 32.5 feet in January 1911. Mount Shasta, California, had the most snowfall in a single storm, with 15.75 feet falling in February 13–19, 1959. The most snow in twenty-four hours was a snowfall of 6.3 feet at Silver Lake, Colorado, on April 14–15, 1921.

World's heaviest hailstone

GOPALGANJ, BANGLADESH

Violent hailstorms often lead to smashed windows in homes, buildings, and cars. But on April 14, 1986, the people of the Gopalganj area of Bangladesh were bombarded with exceptionally powerful hailstones that weighed over 2 pounds, the heaviest ever known. It's reported that ninety-two people were killed. This was the strongest hailstorm on record since April 30, 1888, when a hailstorm struck Moradabad, in the Indian state of Uttar Pradesh. Hailstones the size of cricket balls killed 246 people and more than 1,600 head of livestock. They might not have been the heaviest hailstones, like those in Bangladesh, but they were certainly the deadliest.

MAWSYNRAM

Mawsynram is a cluster of villages in the Khasi Hills of India. The plateau on which they sit overlooks the vast flatlands of Bangladesh. With 467.4 inches of rain falling each year on average, Mawsynram is considered to be the wettest place on Earth. Life here is not without its problems. Wooden bridges are washed away frequently, so locals build living bridges of knotted and interwoven roots of Indian rubber trees. Some people use a traditional "knup" umbrella in the heavy rains. Woven from reeds, this keeps the whole body dry.

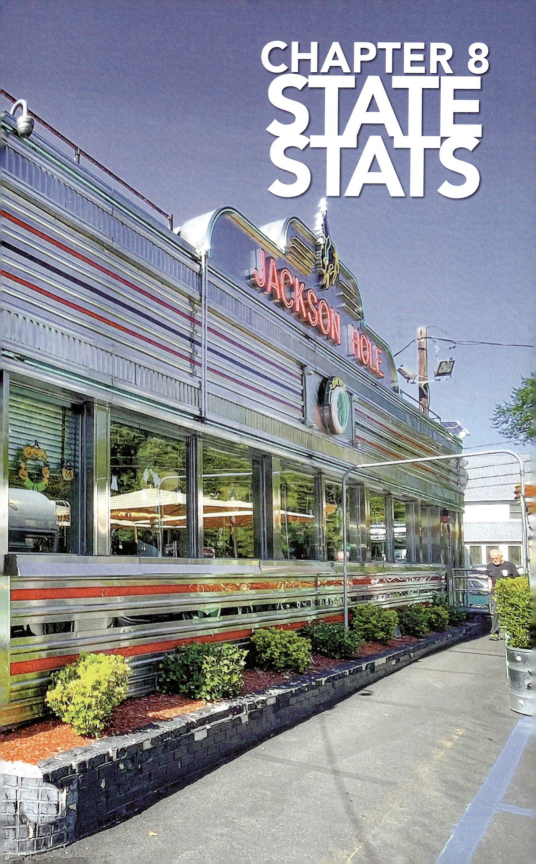

CHAPTER 8
STATE STATS

trending

BLUEBERRY BARRENS MAINE'S
SWEET HARVEST DRAWS THOUSANDS

Wild blueberries grow naturally from North Carolina to Canada and particularly thrive in the acidic soils of Maine. Each year in late summer, thousands of workers from as far afield as Central America and the Caribbean descend upon the state, staying in one of several company-owned camps in the middle of the "blueberry barrens," as these 46,000-odd acres of fields are called, to help harvest them.

A GHOSTLY LEGACY NEVADA'S
EMPTY MINING TOWNS Nevada's mining history began in 1849 when Abner Blackburn struck gold in the Western desert. Ten years later, the Comstock Lode—one of the richest silver strikes in history—was discovered. New towns sprung up throughout Nevada. When the mine in one town dried up, residents moved to the next, and so it continued until the early twentieth century, when the mines finally closed. Today, Nevada is home to around 600 ghost towns.

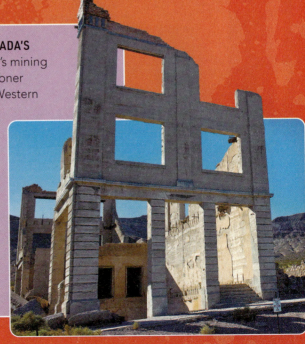

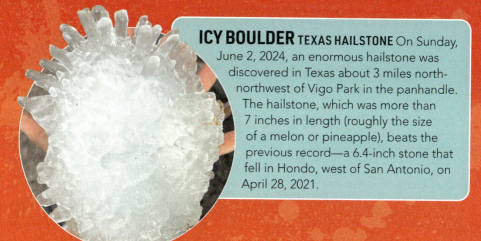

ICY BOULDER TEXAS HAILSTONE

On Sunday, June 2, 2024, an enormous hailstone was discovered in Texas about 3 miles north-northwest of Vigo Park in the panhandle. The hailstone, which was more than 7 inches in length (roughly the size of a melon or pineapple), beats the previous record—a 6.4-inch stone that fell in Hondo, west of San Antonio, on April 28, 2021.

ANIMAL OVERPASS THE LONGEST WILDLIFE CROSSING IN THE WORLD

According to statistics, there are more than 50,000 wildlife–vehicle collisions in California every year. Almost all of them are fatal for the animals (primarily deer, of which an estimated 48,000 die annually). To address this, authorities in California are building the world's longest wildlife crossing—a 210-foot-long bridge that will cross over eight lanes of Highway 101 in Los Angeles County and provide a safe crossing point for a variety of animals. Work on the crossing will be completed in 2026.

TOP BANANA VIRAL FRUIT ART AT NY AUCTION

An artwork by artist Maurizio Cattelan has been a conversation starter since it debuted at Art Basel Miami Beach in December 2019. It made global headlines again when it was sold at auction at Sotheby's in New York in November 2024. The artwork—a yellow banana (bought for 35 cents on the day of the auction) taped to a wall 63 inches above the floor—was subject to a bidding war and eventually was sold for a staggering $6.2 million.

State with the oldest Mardi Gras celebration

ALABAMA

French settlers held the first American Mardi Gras in Mobile, Alabama, in 1703. Yearly celebrations continued until the Civil War and began again in 1866. Today, around one million people gather in the city during the vibrant two-week festival. Dozens of parades with colorful floats and marching bands wind through the streets each day. Partygoers attend masked balls and other lively events sponsored by the city's social societies. On Mardi Gras, which means "Fat Tuesday" in French, six parades continue the party until the stroke of midnight, which marks the end of the year's festivities and the beginning of Lent.

ALASKA

With a total population of 734,000 people and a Native American population exceeding 115,000, Alaska is the state with the highest number of Native Americans per capita—nearly one in six. Alaska is also the state with the highest number of tribal areas, having more than 200 Native villages in total. Among the great Indigenous tribes of Alaska are the Aleut, the Yup'ik, the Eyak, and the Inuit. While most live in modern communities, each tribe continues to uphold the traditions of its elders.

World's largest collection of fossilized poop

ARIZONA

In the quiet Arizona town of Williams, an hour's drive south of the Grand Canyon, a museum dedicated to all manner of ancient poo specimens houses the world's largest collection of coprolites (fossilized poop). The aptly named Poozeum is owned by George Frandsen and holds around 8,000 dollops of dung from creatures as small as termites and as large as *T. rexes*. Not only is the size of the collection a Guinness World Record, but it also contains the world's largest carnivore coprolite—a whopper measuring 2 feet by 2.5 inches and weighing as much as 20 pounds.

ARKANSAS

Only state where diamonds are mined

Crater of Diamonds, near Murfreesboro, Arkansas, is the only active public diamond mine in the United States. Farmer and former owner John Wesley Huddleston first discovered diamonds there in August 1906, and a diamond rush overwhelmed the area after he sold the property to a mining company. For a time, there were two competing mines in this area, but in 1969 General Earth Minerals bought both mines to run them as private tourist attractions. Since 1972, the land has been owned by the state of Arkansas, which designated the area as Crater of Diamonds State Park. Visitors can pay a fee to search through plowed fields in the hope of discovering a gem for themselves.

Almost one hundred years since it first opened its doors to the public, the Los Angeles Hollywood Bowl remains the largest natural outdoor amphitheater in the United States. The summer home of both the Los Angeles Philharmonic and the Hollywood Bowl Orchestra has a capacity for approximately 17,000 people. Many bring picnics and blankets to make the most of their music-filled summer evenings under the stars. Several events have drawn record crowds, including the Beatles, who attracted 18,700 fans in 1964, and Chris Tomlin, whose 2019 performance was a sellout. The highest attendance record of all time goes to the French singer Lily Pons, whose 1936 performance drew an incredible 26,410 people.

State with the largest natural amphitheater

CALIFORNIA

COLORADO

Colorado is currently home to around 280,000 elk, making it the state with the largest elk population. Elk live on both public and private land across the state, from the mountainous regions to lower terrain. Popular targets for hunting, these creatures are regulated by both the Colorado Parks and Wildlife department and the National Park Service. Many elk live within the boundaries of Colorado's Rocky Mountain National Park. Elk are among the largest members of the deer family, and the males—called bulls—are distinguishable by their majestic antlers.

Only state to manufacture PEZ candy

CONNECTICUT

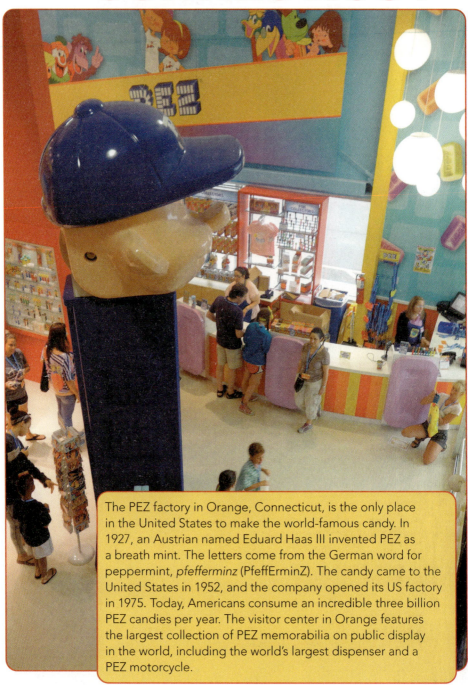

The PEZ factory in Orange, Connecticut, is the only place in the United States to make the world-famous candy. In 1927, an Austrian named Eduard Haas III invented PEZ as a breath mint. The letters come from the German word for peppermint, *pfefferminz* (PfeffErminZ). The candy came to the United States in 1952, and the company opened its US factory in 1975. Today, Americans consume an incredible three billion PEZ candies per year. The visitor center in Orange features the largest collection of PEZ memorabilia on public display in the world, including the world's largest dispenser and a PEZ motorcycle.

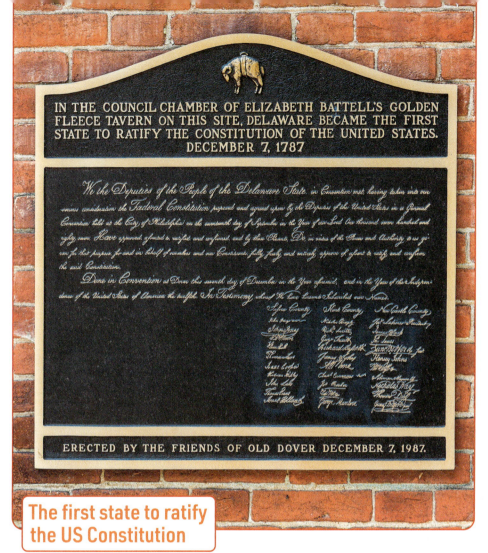

IN THE COUNCIL CHAMBER OF ELIZABETH BATTELL'S GOLDEN FLEECE TAVERN ON THIS SITE, DELAWARE BECAME THE FIRST STATE TO RATIFY THE CONSTITUTION OF THE UNITED STATES. DECEMBER 7, 1787

ERECTED BY THE FRIENDS OF OLD DOVER DECEMBER 7, 1987.

The first state to ratify the US Constitution

DELAWARE

On December 7, 1787, Delaware became the first state to ratify the US Constitution. This was the new federal framework that followed the American Revolutionary War of 1775–1783. Delaware had been one of thirteen colonies fighting the British in the war, hoping to gain independence from British rule. After the war, which the colonies won, the newly independent states needed to form a unified government and the US Constitution was drawn up, setting out the rules they agreed to follow. When delegates from Dover ratified the constitution in 1787, they sealed Delaware's reputation as "The First State," setting a model for other states to follow. Today, Delawareans celebrate Delaware Day on December 7 each year, commemorating their state's trailblazing role in the founding of the United States.

Only state in which alligators and crocodiles live side by side

FLORIDA

Where else but Everglades National Park might you expect to see both alligators and crocodiles living in the wild? The alligator is the more common of the two in America. According to the Florida tourist office, "If you don't see one during an Everglades visit, you're doing something wrong." The American crocodile is endangered, and so a rarer find. Both species like to bask in the sun on the banks of mangrove swamps and other bodies of water. The best way to tell the difference between the two is to check the shape of the snout. An alligator has a more U-shaped snout; a crocodile's is shaped more like a V. And did you know? Not only is Florida the only *state* where you can see alligators and crocodiles, it's also the only place in the *world*!

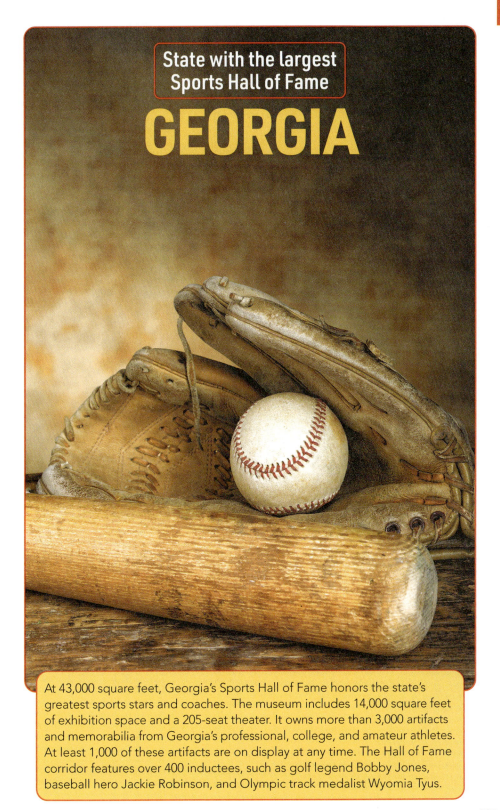

GEORGIA

At 43,000 square feet, Georgia's Sports Hall of Fame honors the state's greatest sports stars and coaches. The museum includes 14,000 square feet of exhibition space and a 205-seat theater. It owns more than 3,000 artifacts and memorabilia from Georgia's professional, college, and amateur athletes. At least 1,000 of these artifacts are on display at any time. The Hall of Fame corridor features over 400 inductees, such as golf legend Bobby Jones, baseball hero Jackie Robinson, and Olympic track medalist Wyomia Tyus.

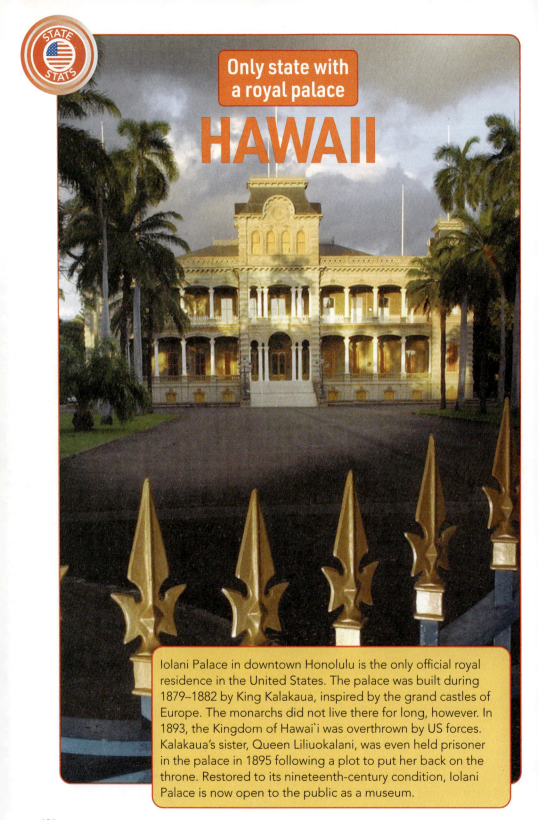

Only state with a royal palace

HAWAII

Iolani Palace in downtown Honolulu is the only official royal residence in the United States. The palace was built during 1879–1882 by King Kalakaua, inspired by the grand castles of Europe. The monarchs did not live there for long, however. In 1893, the Kingdom of Hawai`i was overthrown by US forces. Kalakaua's sister, Queen Liliuokalani, was even held prisoner in the palace in 1895 following a plot to put her back on the throne. Restored to its nineteenth-century condition, Iolani Palace is now open to the public as a museum.

IDAHO

First state with a blue football field

Boise State's Albertsons Stadium, originally dubbed the "Smurf Turf" and now nicknamed "The Blue," was the first blue football field in the United States. In 1986, when the time came to upgrade the old turf, athletics director Gene Bleymaier realized that they would be spending a lot of money on the new field, yet most spectators wouldn't notice the difference. So he asked AstroTurf to create the new field in the school's colors. Since the field's creation, students at the school have consistently voted for blue turf each time the field has been upgraded. Today, nine teams play on a colored playing field, including the Coastal Carolina Chanticleers, whose teal field is dubbed the "Surf Turf."

State with the oldest free public zoo

ILLINOIS

Lincoln Park Zoo, in Chicago, Illinois, remains the oldest free public zoo in the United States. Founded in 1868—just nine years after the Philadelphia Zoo, the country's oldest zoo overall—Lincoln Park Zoo does not charge admission fees. More than two-thirds of the money for the zoo's operating budget comes from food, retail, parking, and fundraisers. Nonetheless, the zoo continues to grow. In October 2021, it opened a new exhibit—the Pepper Family Wildlife Center— a savanna-style habitat that is home to a pride of African lions.

First professional baseball league game

INDIANA

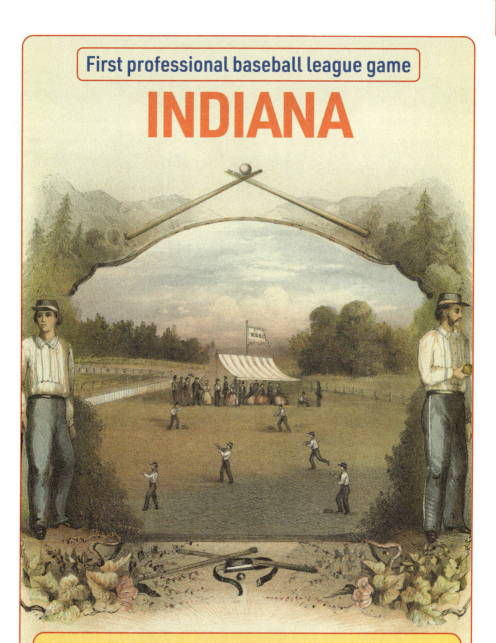

On May 4, 1871, the first National Association professional baseball league game took place on Hamilton Field in Fort Wayne, Indiana. The home team, the Kekiongas, took on the Forest Citys of Cleveland, beating them 2–0 against the odds. The Kekiongas were a little-known team at the time. In fact, the first National Association game had been scheduled to take place between two better-known teams, the Washington Olympics and the Cincinnati Red Stockings, in Washington, DC, on May 3. Heavy rain forced a cancellation, however, and so history was made at Fort Wayne the following day.

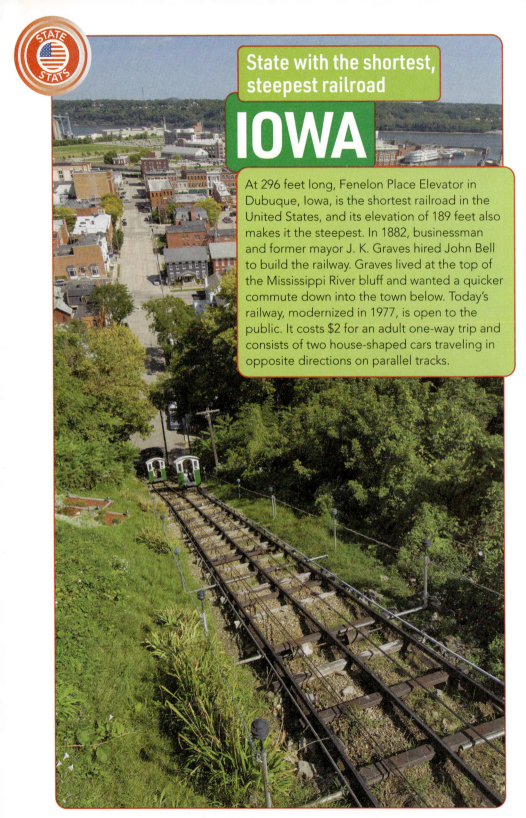

State with the shortest, steepest railroad

IOWA

At 296 feet long, Fenelon Place Elevator in Dubuque, Iowa, is the shortest railroad in the United States, and its elevation of 189 feet also makes it the steepest. In 1882, businessman and former mayor J. K. Graves hired John Bell to build the railway. Graves lived at the top of the Mississippi River bluff and wanted a quicker commute down into the town below. Today's railway, modernized in 1977, is open to the public. It costs $2 for an adult one-way trip and consists of two house-shaped cars traveling in opposite directions on parallel tracks.

Only tallgrass prairie national park

KANSAS

At just 60 miles wide, Flint Hills, Kansas's Tallgrass Prairie National Preserve, is the only US national park dedicated to this ecosystem. Due to plowing by farmers who use the fertile ground to plant crops, the ecosystem is in danger of disappearing worldwide. It has survived in Flint Hills partly because the landscape is not suitable for plowing. The tallgrass prairie contains more than 500 plant species, including different types of grasses—notably Indian grass and big bluestem. In 2009, bison were reintroduced to the preserve in Kansas, and the herd has since grown to about 100 strong.

State with the biggest fireworks display

KENTUCKY

The Kentucky Derby is the longest-running sporting event in the United States. It's also accompanied by the biggest fireworks display held annually in the United States—"Thunder Over Louisville"—which kicks off the racing festivities. Zambelli Fireworks, the display's creator, says that the show requires nearly 60 tons of fireworks shells and a massive 700 miles of wire cable to sync the fireworks to music. The theme for the 2024 show was "Celebrating Derby 150," in honor of the fact that the 150th Kentucky Derby was run that year.

LOUISIANA

Louisiana's Lake Pontchartrain Causeway isn't just the longest bridge in the United States—it's the longest continuous bridge over water anywhere in the world! At 24 miles long, it is supported by a whopping 9,500 concrete pilings. The bridge opened on August 30, 1956, and joins the cities of Mandeville and Metairie. Residents were outraged in 2011 when the causeway's title of longest bridge over water was challenged by a new build in China. But while the Jiaozhou Bay Bridge is longer, it is not entirely over water, so the people of New Orleans lobbied for a more specific award for their causeway—the longest *continuous* bridge over water.

State with the oldest state fair

MAINE

In January 1819, the Somerset Central Agricultural Society sponsored the first-ever Skowhegan State Fair. In the 1800s, state fairs were important places for farmers to gather and learn about new agricultural methods and equipment. After Maine became a state in 1820, the fair continued to grow in size and popularity, gaining its official name in 1942. Today, the Skowhegan State Fair welcomes more than 7,000 exhibitors and 100,000 visitors. Enthusiasts can watch events that include livestock competitions, tractor pulling, a demolition derby, and much more during the ten-day show.

MARYLAND

The Maryland State House in Annapolis is both the oldest capitol building in continuous legislative use and the only statehouse to have once been used as the national capitol. The Continental Congress met there from 1783 to 1784, and it was where George Washington formally resigned as commander in chief of the army following the American Revolution. The current building is the third to be erected on that site and was actually incomplete when the Continental Congress met there in 1783, despite the cornerstone being laid in 1772. The interior of the building was finished in 1797, but not without tragedy—plasterer Thomas Dance fell to his death while working on the dome in 1793.

OLDEST CAPITOL BUILDINGS IN 2025
Age of building (year work was started)

State capitol building

Maryland, 253 years		1772
Virginia, 240 years		1785
New Jersey, 233 years		1792
Massachusetts, 230 years		1795
New Hampshire, 209 years		1816

25 50 75 100 125 150 175 200 225 250
Years

State with the oldest
Thanksgiving celebration

MASSACHUSETTS

The first Thanksgiving celebration took place in 1621, in Plymouth, Massachusetts, when the Pilgrims and the Native Wampanoag people shared a feast. While the celebration became widespread in the Northeast in the late-seventeenth century, Thanksgiving was not celebrated nationally until 1863, when magazine editor Sarah Josepha Hale's writings convinced President Abraham Lincoln to make it a national holiday. Today, Plymouth, Massachusetts, holds a weekend-long celebration honoring its history: the America's Hometown Thanksgiving Celebration.

MICHIGAN

Michigan is home to more than 120 lighthouses! This is hardly surprising, given that Michigan is surrounded by four of the five Great Lakes and has about 3,288 miles of coastline. As many as 1,500 lighthouses were built in the United States—most of them in the early twentieth century. They are somewhat redundant today, because modern lighthouses now use technology to safely guide boats into harbors at night. But without these old lighthouses, many ships would have scuppered on the craggy rocks.

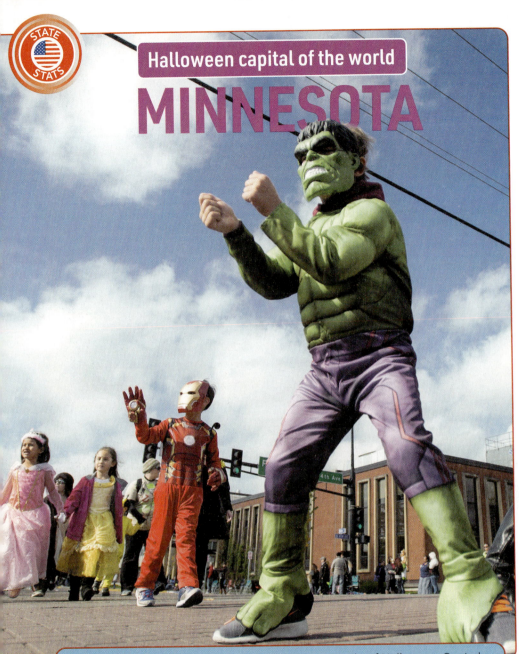

Halloween capital of the world
MINNESOTA

The city of Anoka, Minnesota, proudly proclaims its title of Halloween Capital of the World. Anoka held its first celebration in 1920, when residents organized a costume parade and party, and it has gone all out for the spooky season ever since—except for two years during World War II. Now Halloween in Anoka is a monthlong festival that includes the parade, a house-decorating contest, a "ghost run," and more. In 2022, Anoka fittingly made the news for being the home of the world's largest (and heaviest) jack-o'-lantern: Local pumpkin grower Travis Gienger's 2,560-pound creation was named Maverick and decorated with an eagle, inspired by the movie *Top Gun*.

MISSISSIPPI

Every four years, Jackson, Mississippi, hosts the USA International Ballet Competition, a two-week Olympic-style event that awards gold, silver, and bronze medals. The most recent one was held here in 2023. The competition began in 1964 in Varna, Bulgaria, and rotated among the cities of Varna; Moscow, Russia; and Tokyo, Japan. In June 1979, the competition came to the United States for the first time, and in 1982 Congress passed a joint resolution designating Jackson as the official home of the competition. Dancers vie for prizes and a chance to join ballet companies.

America's first ice-cream cone

MISSOURI

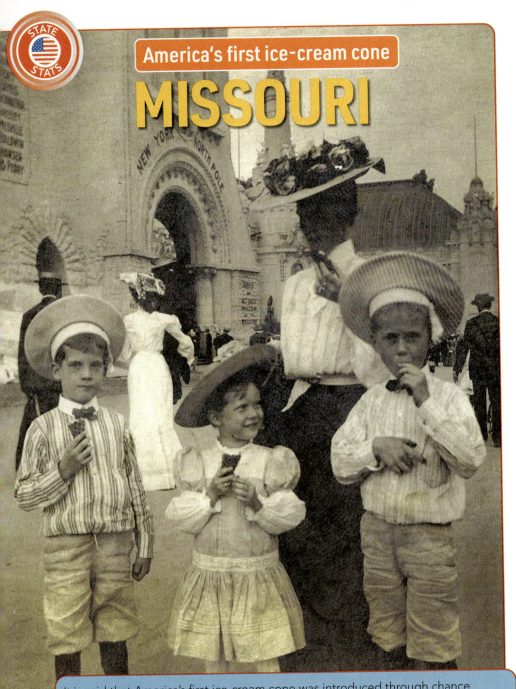

It is said that America's first ice-cream cone was introduced through chance inspiration at the St. Louis World's Fair in 1904. According to the most popular story, a Syrian salesman named Ernest Hamwi saw that an ice-cream vendor had plenty of ice cream but not enough cups and spoons to serve it. Seeing that a neighboring vendor was selling waffle cookies, Hamwi took a cookie and rolled it into a cone for holding ice cream. An immediate success, Hamwi's invention was hailed by vendors as a "cornucopia"—an exotic word for a "cone."

State with the most *T. rex* specimens

MONTANA

The first *Tyrannosaurus rex* fossil ever found was discovered in Montana—paleontologist Barnum Brown excavated it in the Hell Creek Formation in 1902. Since then, many major *T. rex* finds have been made in Montana—from the "Wankel Rex," discovered in 1988, to "Trix," unearthed in 2013, and "Tufts-Love Rex," discovered in 2016. This last was found about 20 percent intact at the site in the Hell Creek Formation. In recent years, a new exhibit named "Dinosaurs Under the Big Sky" has been installed in the Siebel Dinosaur Complex at the Museum of the Rockies in Bozeman, Montana. It is among the biggest and most updated dinosaur exhibits in the world.

NEBRASKA

According to the state's trade office, Nebraska makes around 300 million pounds of popcorn every year—accounting for more than 30 percent of all popcorn produced in the United States. Popcorn is an American favorite. Every year, Americans eat enough popcorn to fill up the Empire State Building eighteen times! Nebraska is particularly good at growing corn due to its irrigation systems and sandy loam soil, which provide ideal conditions for around 67,000 acres of cornfields. While some other states, such as Indiana, sometimes plant more acreage of corn, Nebraska's conditions usually produce a higher yield.

NEVADA

State with the most wild horses

The largest herd of wild horses left in the United States makes its home in the state of Nevada. The Bureau of Land Management (BLM) believes that there are 73,520 wild horses and burros in the American West, with around half of those roaming in Nevada—33,338, according to a 2024 estimate. Around 800 of these horses live on the Nevada Wild Horse Range, the first wild horse range in the country. Sadly, BLM statistics show that the wild horse population—in both Nevada and across the United States—is in decline, so herd management and conservation are important causes to the people of Nevada.

State with the oldest skiing club

NEW HAMPSHIRE

Nansen Ski Club, in Milan, New Hampshire, was founded by Norwegian immigrants in 1872, making it the oldest continuously operating skiing club in the United States. When it first opened, the venue accepted only other Scandinavians living in the area, but it was then made available to everyone as more skiing enthusiasts began to move into New Hampshire from Quebec to work in the mills there. For fifty years, the club was home to the largest ski jump east of the Mississippi, and the ski jump was used for Olympic tryouts.

NEW JERSEY

The state of New Jersey has more than five hundred diners, earning it the title of Diner Capital of the World. The state has a higher concentration of diners than anywhere else in the United States. They are such an iconic part of the state's identity that, in 2016, a New Jersey diners exhibit opened at the Middlesex County Museum, showcasing the history of the diner, from early twentieth-century lunch cars to modern roadside spots. The state has many different types of diners, including famous restaurant-style eateries like Tops Diner in East Newark, as well as retro hole-in-the-wall diners with jukeboxes and booths.

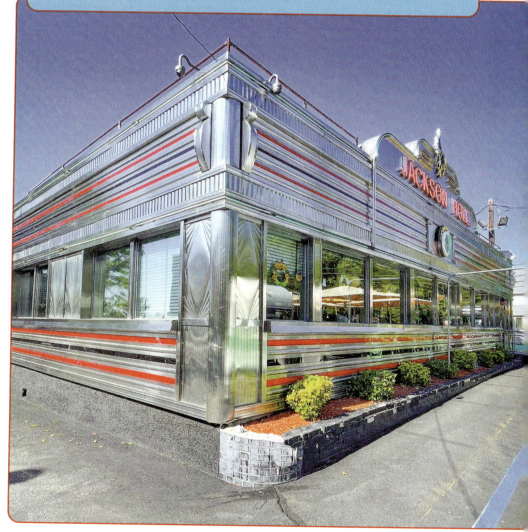

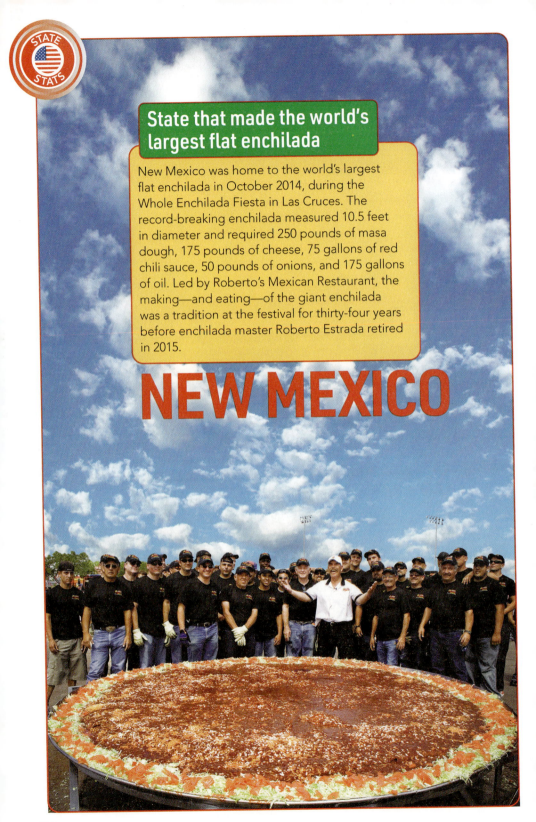

State that made the world's largest flat enchilada

New Mexico was home to the world's largest flat enchilada in October 2014, during the Whole Enchilada Fiesta in Las Cruces. The record-breaking enchilada measured 10.5 feet in diameter and required 250 pounds of masa dough, 175 pounds of cheese, 75 gallons of red chili sauce, 50 pounds of onions, and 175 gallons of oil. Led by Roberto's Mexican Restaurant, the making—and eating—of the giant enchilada was a tradition at the festival for thirty-four years before enchilada master Roberto Estrada retired in 2015.

NEW MEXICO

The smallest church in America, Oneida's Cross Island Chapel, measures 81 by 51 inches and has just enough room for the minister and two churchgoers. Built in 1989, the church is in an odd location, in the middle of a pond. The simple, whitewashed clapboard chapel stands on a little jetty that has moorings for a boat or two. The island that the chapel is named for barely breaks the surface of the water nearby and is simply a craggy pile of rock bearing a cross.

America's smallest church

NEW YORK

State with the largest private house

NORTH CAROLINA

LARGEST PRIVATE HOUSES IN THE UNITED STATES
Area in square feet

Private house	Square feet
Biltmore Estate, Asheville, NC	175,000
Oheka Castle, Huntington, NY	109,000
The One, Bel Air, CA	105,000
Arden House, Harriman, NY	100,000
Whitehall, Palm Beach, FL	100,000

The Biltmore Estate, in the mountains of Asheville, North Carolina, is home to Biltmore House, the largest privately owned house in the United States. George Vanderbilt commissioned the 250-room French Renaissance–style chateau in 1889 and opened it to his friends and family as a country retreat in 1895. Designed by architect Richard Morris Hunt, Biltmore House has an impressive thirty-five bedrooms and forty-three bathrooms, and boasts a floor space of over 4 acres. In 1930, the Vanderbilt family opened Biltmore House to the public.

Biggest honey producer

NORTH DAKOTA

In the production of honey, North Dakota outstrips all other US states year after year. According to the USDA's National Agricultural Statistics Service, the state's 520,000 honey-producing colonies each yield an average 60 pounds of the sweet stuff per year. It seems the North Dakota climate is just right for honeybees and—more importantly—for the flowers from which they collect their nectar. Typical summer weather features warm days but cool nights.

OHIO

NO SELF RESPECTING WOMAN SHOULD WISH OR WORK FOR THE SUCCESS OF A PARTY THAT IGNORES HER SEX

In the 1800s, working conditions in US factories were grueling and pay was very low. Most of the workers were women, and it was not uncommon for them to work for twelve to fourteen hours a day, six days a week. The factories were not heated or air-conditioned, and there was no compensation for being sick. By the 1850s, several organizations had formed to improve the working conditions for women and to shorten their workday. In 1852, Ohio passed a law limiting the working day to ten hours for women under the age of eighteen. It was a small step, but it was also the first act of legislation of its kind in the United States.

Only US state capitol with an oil well beneath it

OKLAHOMA

The Oklahoma State Capitol has one very unique feature: an oil well! Affectionately named "Petunia #1" because it was built by drilling at an angle through a flower bed, it was a working well from 1942 to 1986, producing more than 1.5 million barrels of oil by the time it dried up. The bottom of the well sits about 1.25 miles under the capitol building, and visitors can see it as part of the capitol tour. Petunia #1 was once one of more than twenty similar wells on capitol grounds, which are situated on the Oklahoma City Oil Field, but its rig is now the only one to remain in place, preserved as a historic monument.

OREGON

World's largest cinnamon roll

Wolferman's Bakery holds the record for the largest cinnamon roll ever made. The spiced confection measured 9 feet long and was topped with 147 pounds of cream cheese frosting. It was made to celebrate the launch of the bakery's new 5-pound cinnamon roll. Using its popular recipe, Wolferman's needed 20 pounds of eggs, 350 pounds of flour, 378 pounds of cinnamon-sugar filling, and no fewer than 220 cinnamon sticks in their scaled-up version. The 1,150-pound cinnamon roll was transported to Medford's Annual Pear Blossom Festival in south Oregon, where visitors snapped it up for $2 a slice.

State that manufactures the most crayons
PENNSYLVANIA

Easton, Pennsylvania, is home to the Crayola crayon factory and has been the company's headquarters since 1976. The factory produces an amazing twelve million crayons every single day, made from uncolored paraffin and pigment powder. In 1996, the company opened the Crayola Experience in downtown Easton. The Experience includes a live interactive show during which guests can watch a "crayonologist" make crayons, just as they are made at the factory nearby.

State with the oldest Fourth of July celebration

RHODE ISLAND

Bristol, Rhode Island, holds America's longest continuously running Fourth of July celebration. The idea for the celebration came from Revolutionary War veteran Rev. Henry Wight, of Bristol's First Congregational Church, who organized "Patriotic Exercises" to honor the nation's founders and those who fought to establish the United States. Today, Bristol begins celebrating the holiday on June 14, and puts on an array of events leading up to the Fourth itself—including free concerts, a baseball game, a Fourth of July Ball, and a half-marathon.

SOUTH CAROLINA

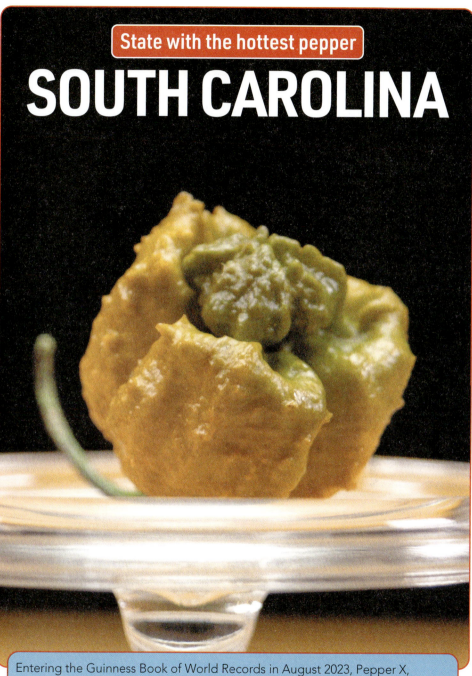

Entering the Guinness Book of World Records in August 2023, Pepper X, created by Smokin' Ed Currie of Rock Hill, South Carolina, is officially the hottest pepper in the world, measuring an average of 2.7 million Scoville heat units (SHU). To get a feel for how hot that is, just know that a regular jalapeño clocks in at 2,500–8,000 SHU. Currie also created a previous record holder, the Carolina Reaper, which held the record from 2013 to 2023, and measures an average of 1.64 million SHU.

State with the largest sculpture

SOUTH DAKOTA

While South Dakota is famous as the home of Mount Rushmore, it is also the location of another giant mountain carving: the Crazy Horse Memorial. The mountain carving, which is still in progress, will be the largest sculpture in the world when it is completed, at 563 feet tall and 641 feet long. Korczak Ziolkowski, who worked on Mount Rushmore, began the carving in 1948 to pay tribute to Crazy Horse—the Lakota leader who defeated General Custer at the Battle of the Little Bighorn. More than seventy years later, Ziolkowski's family continues his work, relying completely on funding from visitors and donors.

TENNESSEE

State that makes all the MoonPies

Tennessee is the home of the MoonPie, which was conceived there in 1917 by bakery salesman Earl Mitchell Sr. after a group of local miners asked for a filling treat "as big as the moon." Made from marshmallow, graham crackers, and chocolate, the sandwich cookies were soon being mass-produced at Tennessee's Chattanooga Bakery, and MoonPie was registered as a trademark by the bakery in 1919. MoonPies first sold at just five cents each and quickly became popular—even being named the official snack of NASCAR in the late 1990s. Today, Chattanooga Bakery makes around a million MoonPies every day.

Only state with a breeding population of wild ocelots

TEXAS

There are thought to be fewer than 100 wild ocelots in the United States today, making them federally endangered. These cats call South Texas their home. Members of the subspecies *Leopardus pardalis albescens* mostly live in dedicated wildlife corridors on Texas's southeastern coast, near the Gulf of Mexico. A 2024 discovery may give conservationists reason to hope. Researchers studying the DNA of a recently killed ocelot found two genetic markers usually seen in the Mexican population. These markers, not expected in the South Texas ocelots, could suggest a population that has not previously been discovered in the state.

State with the largest saltwater lake

UTAH

The Great Salt Lake, which inspired the name of Utah's largest city, is the largest saltwater lake in the United States, at around 75 miles long and 30 miles wide. Sometimes called "America's Dead Sea," it is typically larger than each of the states of Delaware and Rhode Island. Its size, however, fluctuates as water levels rise and fall. Since 1849, the water level has varied by as much as 23 feet, which can shift the shoreline by up to 15 miles. The Great Salt Lake is too salty to support most aquatic life but is home to several kinds of algae, as well as the brine shrimp that feed on them.

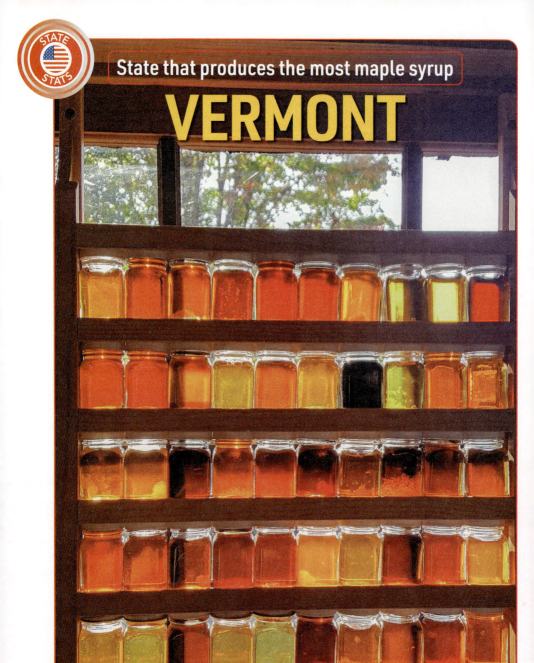

State that produces the most maple syrup

VERMONT

The state of Vermont produced 2.5 million gallons of maple syrup in 2022. The state's highest crop ever, it represents more than 50 percent of the country's total. Vermont's 1,500 maple syrup producers take sap from six million tree taps. They have to collect 40 gallons of maple sap in order to produce just 1 gallon of syrup. Producers also use maple sap for making other treats, such as maple butter, sugar, and candies.

STATE STATS

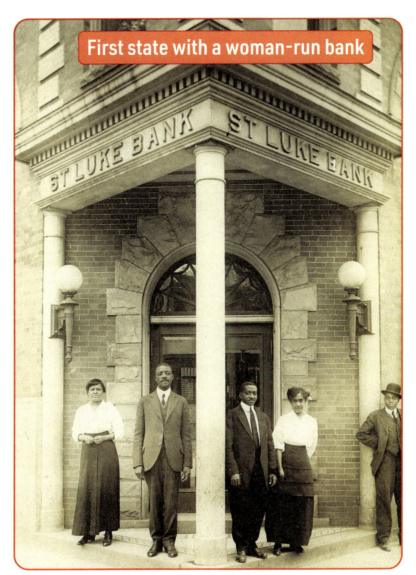

First state with a woman-run bank

VIRGINIA

In 1903, Maggie Lena Walker opened the St. Luke Penny Savings Bank in Richmond, making Virginia the first state with a bank founded and run by a woman. A leading civil activist, Walker was also Black, making her achievement all the more remarkable in a time when the Jim Crow laws did much to restrict the advancement of Black people in the Southern states. Through the bank and other enterprises that included a newspaper and a department store, Walker sought to provide members of the Black community with opportunities to improve their lives through employment, investment, and supporting one another's businesses.

State with the oldest GAS station

WASHINGTON

The Teapot Dome Service Station in Zillah, Washington, was once the oldest working gas station in the United States, and is still the only one built to commemorate a political scandal. Now preserved as a museum, the gas station was built in 1922 as a monument to the Teapot Dome Scandal, in which Albert Fall, President Warren G. Harding's Secretary of the Interior, took bribes to lease government oil reserves to private companies. The gas station, located on Washington's Old Highway 12, was moved in 1978 to make way for Interstate 82, then again in 2007 when the city of Zillah purchased it as a historic landmark.

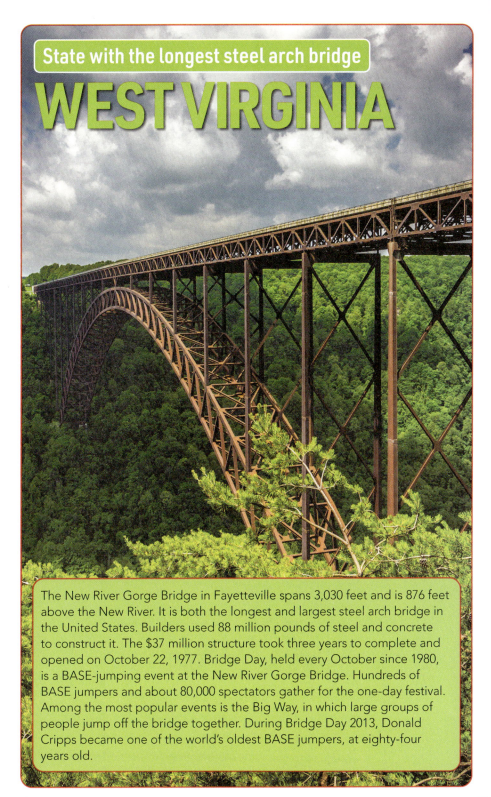

WEST VIRGINIA

The New River Gorge Bridge in Fayetteville spans 3,030 feet and is 876 feet above the New River. It is both the longest and largest steel arch bridge in the United States. Builders used 88 million pounds of steel and concrete to construct it. The $37 million structure took three years to complete and opened on October 22, 1977. Bridge Day, held every October since 1980, is a BASE-jumping event at the New River Gorge Bridge. Hundreds of BASE jumpers and about 80,000 spectators gather for the one-day festival. Among the most popular events is the Big Way, in which large groups of people jump off the bridge together. During Bridge Day 2013, Donald Cripps became one of the world's oldest BASE jumpers, at eighty-four years old.

World's largest aviation event

WISCONSIN

Around 10,000 aircraft and more than 650,000 visitors flock to Oshkosh, Wisconsin, each summer for the Experimental Aircraft Association's annual AirVenture event at Wittman Regional Airport. In 2023, the event included nearly 1,500 vintage planes, more than 1,000 homemade planes, and over 125 seaplanes and amphibious planes, among many other aircraft. The huge number of planes that fly in for this gathering together with AirVenture's daily air shows transform Wittman into the busiest airport in the world for around ten days each year, with nearly 150 takeoffs and landings per hour. The event began in 1953 and was originally held at Milwaukee's Curtiss-Wright Field, now known as Timmerman Airport. Oshkosh also is home to the EAA Aviation Museum.

WYOMING

Grand Prismatic Spring, in the Wyoming section of Yellowstone National Park, is the largest hot spring in the United States. The spring measures 370 feet in diameter and is more than 121 feet deep; Yellowstone National Park says that the spring is bigger than a football field and deeper than a ten-story building. Grand Prismatic is not just the largest spring but also the most photographed thermal feature in Yellowstone due to its bright colors. The colors come from different kinds of bacteria, living in each part of the spring, that thrive at various temperatures. As water comes up from the middle of the spring, it is too hot to support most bacterial life, but as the water spreads out to the edges of the spring, it cools in concentric circles.

CHAPTER 9
SPORTS STARS

THE GOTHLETE VOLLEYBALL PLAYER MAKES WAVES

Boise State beach volleyball player Nora Hayd went viral in 2024 after the Internet got hold of her roster photo. Hayd stands out from her fellow athletes with facial piercings, pink hair, and heavy eyeliner. Commenters online dubbed her the "goth athlete," or "gothlete," for short. The 6-foot-1 player hasn't let the attention get to her and instead is relishing the opportunity to collaborate with some of her favorite brands, Hot Topic included!

BIGGEST LOSERS WHITE SOX BREAK RECORD

In 2024, the Chicago White Sox broke the modern record for most losses in an MLB season. Their 121st loss, to the Detroit Tigers in September, broke the record of 120 set by the 1962 New York Mets. Fans remained in good humor, however. A newspaper poll surveyed fans at 114 losses and found that more than 80 percent of respondents were rooting for them to break the loss record—mostly to force some change!

THE CAITLIN CLARK EFFECT RECORD VIEWING FIGURES FOR WNBA

Aside from the All-Star Game, the top 10 highest viewing figures for the NBA were all for games featuring the Indiana Fever. This is unsurprising, as viewers have flocked to watch the rookie season of Indiana's Caitlin Clark, hailed as one of the greatest players in the history of college basketball. Clark won Rookie of the Year for her impressive first WNBA season. The increased attention the WNBA received has been widely called the "Caitlin Clark Effect."

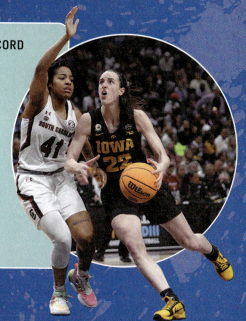

HISTORIC SLAM DUNK WOMEN'S BASKETBALL MAKES ITS MARK

The NCAA women's basketball championship game on April 7, 2024, overtook the men's championship game in views for the first time. It was held at the Rocket Mortgage Field House in Cleveland, Ohio, between the South Carolina Gamecocks and the Iowa Hawkeyes. The game generated over 93.9 million views on social media within a week. South Carolina won 87–75.

SERVING LOOKS VENUS WILLIAMS BARBIE RELEASED

In May 2024, Mattel created nine one-of-a-kind dolls celebrating female athletes and role models for Barbie's sixty-fifth anniversary. Among the sports stars chosen was tennis pro Venus Williams, whose doll wears white tennis clothes and her signature gold earrings. Williams became the first female tennis player to win equal prize money to a male player at Wimbledon in 2007, and her career has included seven major singles titles and fourteen major doubles titles.

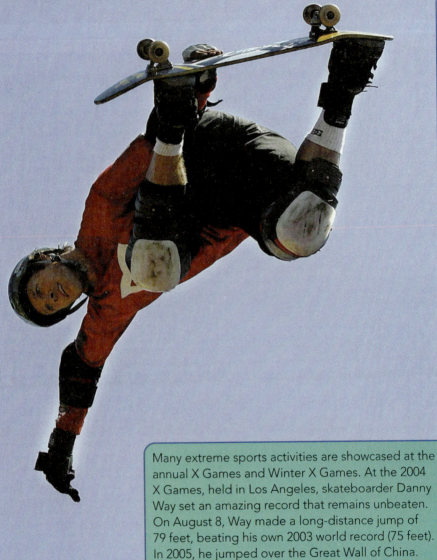

Many extreme sports activities are showcased at the annual X Games and Winter X Games. At the 2004 X Games, held in Los Angeles, skateboarder Danny Way set an amazing record that remains unbeaten. On August 8, Way made a long-distance jump of 79 feet, beating his own 2003 world record (75 feet). In 2005, he jumped over the Great Wall of China. He made the jump despite having torn ligaments in his ankle during a practice jump on the previous day.

World's longest skateboard ramp jump

DANNY WAY

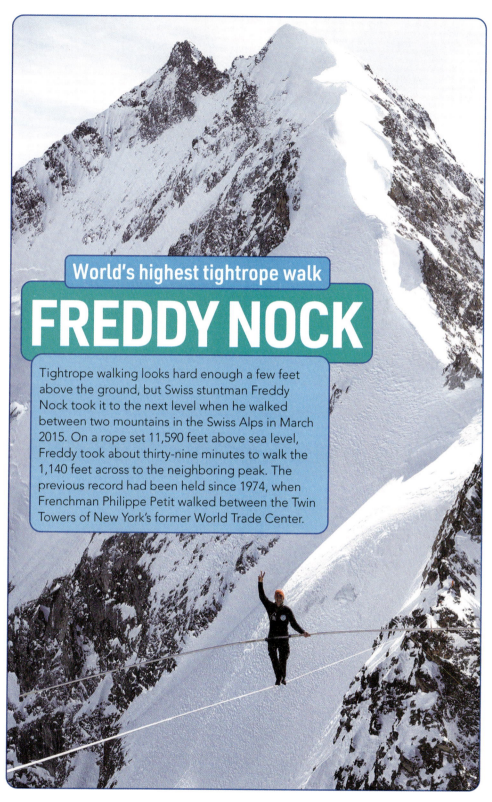

World's highest tightrope walk

FREDDY NOCK

Tightrope walking looks hard enough a few feet above the ground, but Swiss stuntman Freddy Nock took it to the next level when he walked between two mountains in the Swiss Alps in March 2015. On a rope set 11,590 feet above sea level, Freddy took about thirty-nine minutes to walk the 1,140 feet across to the neighboring peak. The previous record had been held since 1974, when Frenchman Philippe Petit walked between the Twin Towers of New York's former World Trade Center.

Most successful BMX rider of all time

MAT HOFFMAN

No one has done more for the sport of BMX than Mat Hoffman. Nicknamed "The Condor," Hoffman is recognized as the greatest Vert rider in the sport, winning the World Vert Championship on ten occasions and also picking up six medals at the X Games. He is also credited with inventing more than 100 tricks, such as the 900 (which he successfully completed in 1989), a no-handed 900, a Flip Faki (a backflip that includes landing backward), and a Flair (a backflip with a 180-degree turn). He also holds the world record for the highest air achieved on a BMX bike over a 24-foot-tall quarterpipe (26.5 feet) and even took his bike BASE jumping off a 3,500-foot cliff in Norway.

World's highest basketball shot

DUDE PERFECT

On April 20, 2023, trick shooters Dude Perfect broke the world record for the highest-ever basketball shot, sinking it from a platform close to the top of iconic STRAT Tower on the Las Vegas Strip. Known locally as the Stratosphere, the tower is 1,149 feet tall, and Dude Perfect's platform was set at 856 feet above the basketball hoop, which was barely visible from above. The team spent twenty-five hours in total over a period of three days before Tyler Toney, one of the team's "dudes," achieved the record-breaking feat. Dude Perfect beat the previous world record—achieved by Australian team How Ridiculous in 2018—by 196 feet.

The only rookie in WNBA history to record a triple-double

CAITLIN CLARK

Iowa-born Caitlin Clark enjoyed a stellar collegiate basketball career with the Iowa Hawkeyes, winning women's national player of the year twice and breaking the NCAA all-time scoring record of any man or woman. After graduating, she was selected first overall by Indiana Fever in the 2024 WNBA Draft. On July 6, 2024, playing against New York Liberty—Clark notched up a headline-grabbing 19 points, 12 rebounds, and 13 assists in an 83–78 victory, becoming the first rookie in WNBA history to achieve a triple-double (a double-digit number in three of the sport's five statistical categories).

WNBA player with the most career points

DIANA TAURASI

After a standout college career and three NCAA championships with the University of Connecticut Huskies, Diana Taurasi joined the Phoenix Mercury in the WNBA in 2004. Her prolific scoring helped the Mercury to its first WNBA title in 2007 (and two more since then), and her international career includes six consecutive Team USA Olympic golds in 2004–2024. Playing mainly as a guard, Taurasi became the all-time leading WNBA scorer in 2017.

MOST CAREER POINTS IN THE WNBA	
Diana Taurasi	10,646
Tina Charles	7,696
Tina Thompson	7,488
DeWanna Bonner	7,482
Tamika Catchings	7,380

First NBA player to reach 40,000 career points

LEBRON JAMES

MOST CAREER POINTS IN THE NBA		
LeBron James	(2003–present)	40,706
Kareem Abdul-Jabbar	(1969–1989)	38,387
Karl Malone	(1985–2004)	36,928
Kobe Bryant	(1996–2016)	33,643
Michael Jordan	(1984–2003)	32,292

On Saturday, March 2, 2024, at age thirty-nine and sixty-two days, LeBron James became the first player in NBA history to reach 40,000 points, after having smashed Kareem Abdul-Jabbar's previous record of 38,387 in 2022. The milestone was set during a game against the Denver Nuggets, and the ball was taken out of play to preserve it for posterity. James's Los Angeles Lakers went on to lose the game 124–114, leaving him with "bittersweet" feelings over his achievement.

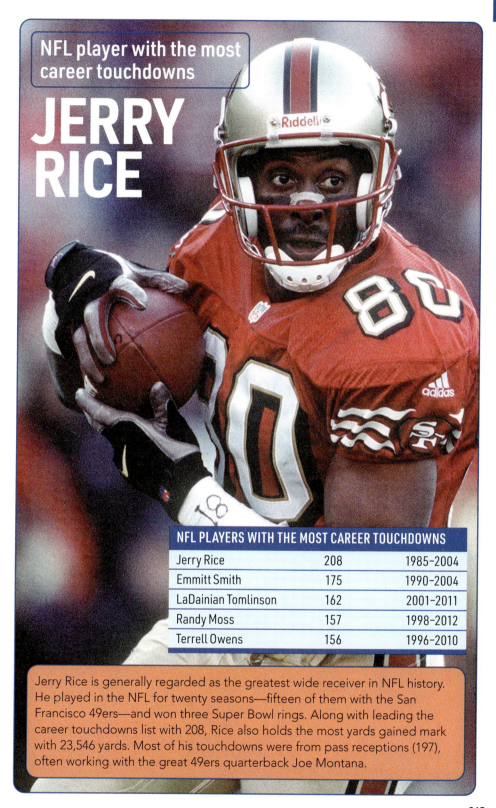

NFL player with the most career touchdowns

JERRY RICE

NFL PLAYERS WITH THE MOST CAREER TOUCHDOWNS

Jerry Rice	208	1985–2004
Emmitt Smith	175	1990–2004
LaDainian Tomlinson	162	2001–2011
Randy Moss	157	1998–2012
Terrell Owens	156	1996–2010

Jerry Rice is generally regarded as the greatest wide receiver in NFL history. He played in the NFL for twenty seasons—fifteen of them with the San Francisco 49ers—and won three Super Bowl rings. Along with leading the career touchdowns list with 208, Rice also holds the most yards gained mark with 23,546 yards. Most of his touchdowns were from pass receptions (197), often working with the great 49ers quarterback Joe Montana.

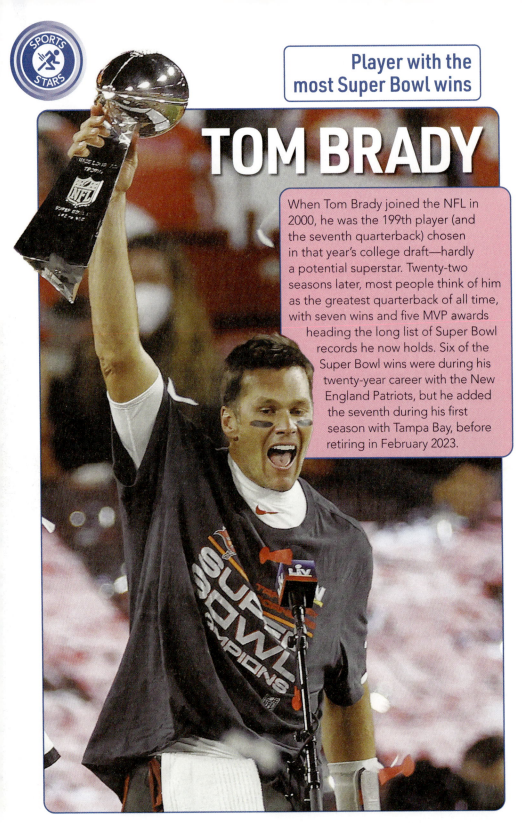

Player with the most Super Bowl wins

TOM BRADY

When Tom Brady joined the NFL in 2000, he was the 199th player (and the seventh quarterback) chosen in that year's college draft—hardly a potential superstar. Twenty-two seasons later, most people think of him as the greatest quarterback of all time, with seven wins and five MVP awards heading the long list of Super Bowl records he now holds. Six of the Super Bowl wins were during his twenty-year career with the New England Patriots, but he added the seventh during his first season with Tampa Bay, before retiring in February 2023.

USC TROJANS

The Rose Bowl is college football's oldest postseason event, first played in 1902. Taking place near January 1 of each year, the game is normally played between the Pac-12 Conference champion and the Big Ten Conference champion, but one year in three, it is part of college football's playoffs. The University of Southern California has easily the best record in the Rose Bowl, with twenty-five wins from thirty-four appearances, followed by the Ohio State Buckeyes (ten wins from seventeen appearances). The Buckeyes took that second spot on the winners' list from the Michigan Wolverines with their 41–21 victory over the Oregon Ducks on January 1, 2025.

MLB team with the most World Series wins

NY YANKEES

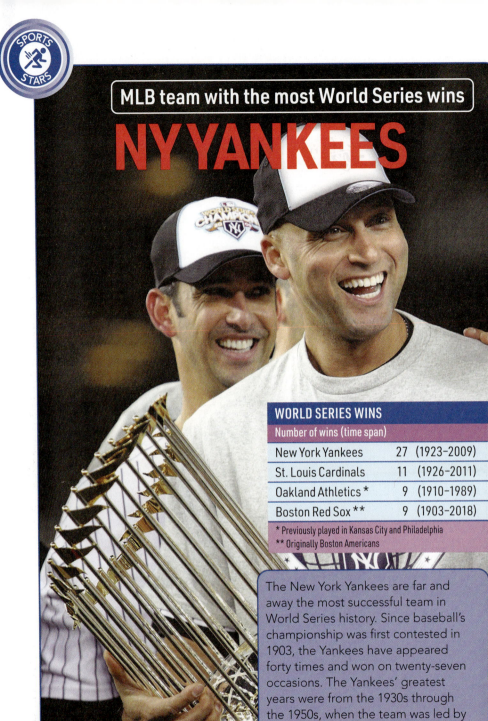

WORLD SERIES WINS

Number of wins (time span)

New York Yankees	27	(1923–2009)
St. Louis Cardinals	11	(1926–2011)
Oakland Athletics *	9	(1910–1989)
Boston Red Sox **	9	(1903–2018)

* Previously played in Kansas City and Philadelphia
** Originally Boston Americans

The New York Yankees are far and away the most successful team in World Series history. Since baseball's championship was first contested in 1903, the Yankees have appeared forty times and won on twenty-seven occasions. The Yankees' greatest years were from the 1930s through the 1950s, when the team was led by legends such as Babe Ruth and Joe DiMaggio. Their nearest challengers are the St. Louis Cardinals from the National League, with eleven wins from nineteen appearances.

CARLOS VELA

Mexican soccer star Carlos Vela made his name while playing for the Spanish team Real Sociedad, which he joined in 2011. During his time there, he scored seventy-three goals in a six-year, 250-match spell, earning a reputation as one of the most gifted strikers of his generation. In 2017, at age twenty-eight, he turned his back on European football to join Los Angeles FC, where he went on to achieve further glory: During the 2019 season, he made fifteen assists and scored an MLS (Major League Soccer) record thirty-four goals.

MOST MLS GOALS IN A SEASON		
Goals	Player	Club, season
34	Carlos Vela	Los Angeles FC, 2019
31	Josef Martínez	Atlanta United FC, 2018
30	Zlatan Ibrahimović	Los Angeles Galaxy, 2019

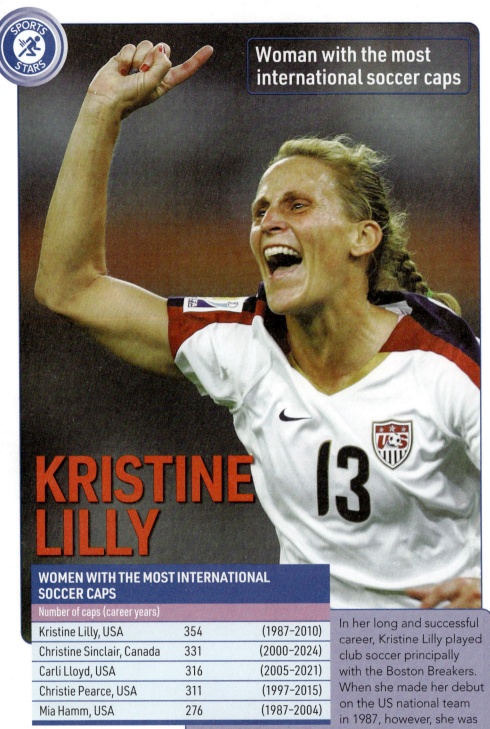

Woman with the most international soccer caps

KRISTINE LILLY

WOMEN WITH THE MOST INTERNATIONAL SOCCER CAPS

Number of caps (career years)		
Kristine Lilly, USA	354	(1987–2010)
Christine Sinclair, Canada	331	(2000–2024)
Carli Lloyd, USA	316	(2005–2021)
Christie Pearce, USA	311	(1997–2015)
Mia Hamm, USA	276	(1987–2004)

In her long and successful career, Kristine Lilly played club soccer principally with the Boston Breakers. When she made her debut on the US national team in 1987, however, she was still in high school. Her total of 354 international caps is the world's highest for a man or woman, and her trophy haul includes two World Cup winner's medals and two Olympic golds.

Country with the most FIFA World Cup wins

BRAZIL

Brazil, host of the 2014 FIFA World Cup, has lifted the trophy the most times in the tournament's history. Germany, second on the list, has more runner-up and semifinal appearances and hence, arguably, a stronger record overall. However, many would say that Brazil's 1970 lineup, led by the incomparable Pelé, ranks as the finest team ever. The host team has won five of the twenty tournaments that have been completed to date.

FIFA WORLD CUP WINNERS		
Number of wins		
Brazil	5	1958, 1962, 1970, 1994, 2002
Germany*	4	1954, 1974, 1990, 2014
Italy	4	1934, 1938, 1982, 2006
Argentina	3	1978, 1986, 2022
Uruguay	2	1930, 1950
France	2	1998, 2018

* As West Germany 1954, 1974

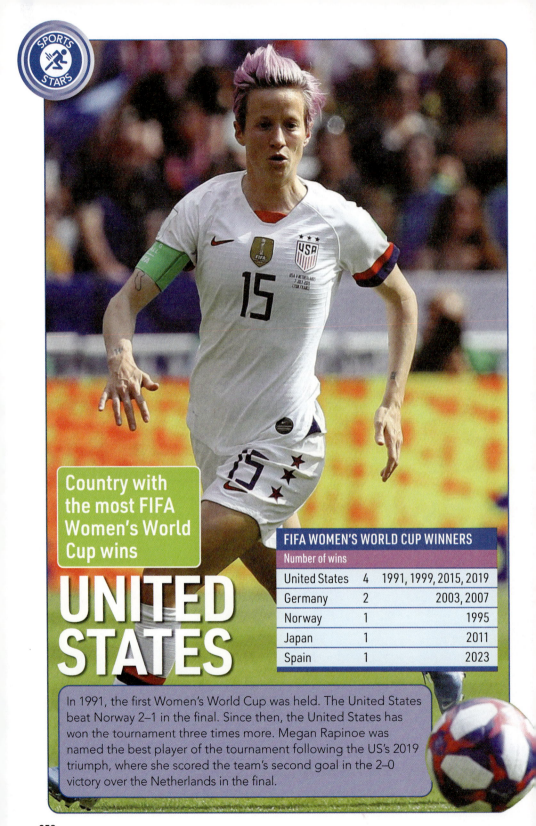

Country with the most FIFA Women's World Cup wins

UNITED STATES

FIFA WOMEN'S WORLD CUP WINNERS		
Number of wins		
United States	4	1991, 1999, 2015, 2019
Germany	2	2003, 2007
Norway	1	1995
Japan	1	2011
Spain	1	2023

In 1991, the first Women's World Cup was held. The United States beat Norway 2–1 in the final. Since then, the United States has won the tournament three times more. Megan Rapinoe was named the best player of the tournament following the US's 2019 triumph, where she scored the team's second goal in the 2–0 victory over the Netherlands in the final.

Most Ballon d'Or wins

LIONEL MESSI

A skilled playmaker, Argentina's Lionel Messi is considered by many to be the greatest soccer player of his generation. Before moving to Inter Miami in 2023 (following two seasons at Paris Saint-Germain), Messi had spent almost his entire career with Barcelona, leading his team to thirty-five trophies. He holds the all-time record for the most La Liga goals (474) and the most international goals by a South American player (112). He is also the only player in the game's history to have won the Ballon d'Or, awarded annually since 1956 to the world's best player, on eight occasions (in 2009, 2010, 2011, 2012, 2015, 2019, 2021, and 2023).

Woman with the most Grand Slams in Open Era

SERENA WILLIAMS

Serena Williams is truly one of the all-time greats in tennis, playing with a combination of power and athleticism that has made her almost unbeatable when she's been at her best. Williams first won a Grand Slam singles title at the US Open in 1999 and has since added five more, plus three in France and seven each in Australia and at Wimbledon.

She's tough to beat in doubles, too. She and her sister Venus Williams have reached fourteen Grand Slam finals together—and won them all.

SERENA WILLIAMS GRAND SLAMS	
Finals wins	
US Open	1999, 2002, 2008, 2012, 2013, 2014
Australian Open	2003, 2005, 2007, 2009, 2010, 2015, 2017
French Open	2002, 2013, 2015
Wimbledon	2002, 2003, 2009, 2010, 2012, 2015, 2016

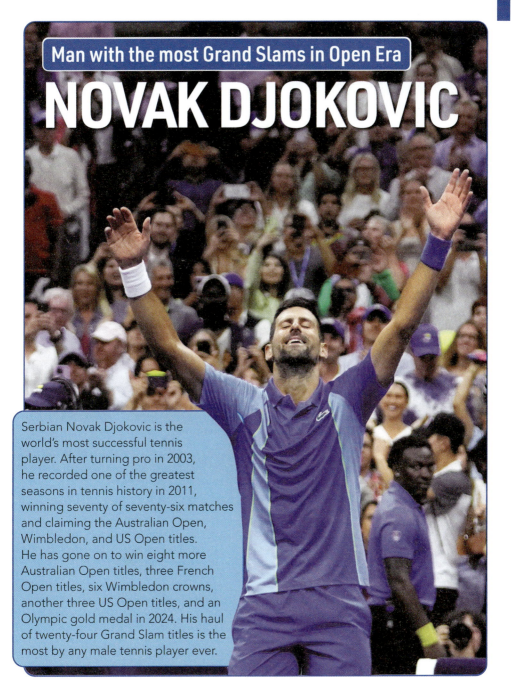

Man with the most Grand Slams in Open Era

NOVAK DJOKOVIC

Serbian Novak Djokovic is the world's most successful tennis player. After turning pro in 2003, he recorded one of the greatest seasons in tennis history in 2011, winning seventy of seventy-six matches and claiming the Australian Open, Wimbledon, and US Open titles. He has gone on to win eight more Australian Open titles, three French Open titles, six Wimbledon crowns, another three US Open titles, and an Olympic gold medal in 2024. His haul of twenty-four Grand Slam titles is the most by any male tennis player ever.

GRAND SLAM TITLES	PLAYERS	AUSTRALIAN OPEN	FRENCH OPEN	WIMBLEDON	US OPEN
24	Novak Djokovic (Serbia, 2008–)	10	3	7	4
22	Rafael Nadal (Spain, 2005–2024)	2	14	2	4
20	Roger Federer (Switzerland, 2003–2018)	6	1	8	5

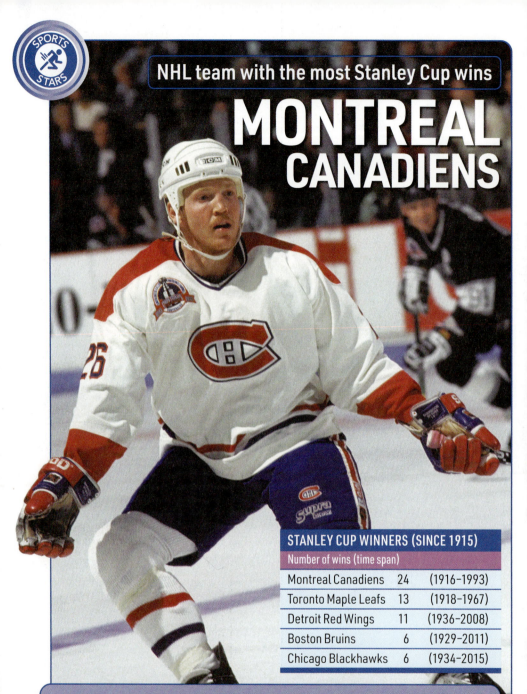

MONTREAL
CANADIENS

SPORTS STARS

STANLEY CUP WINNERS (SINCE 1915)		
Number of wins (time span)		
Montreal Canadiens	24	(1916–1993)
Toronto Maple Leafs	13	(1918–1967)
Detroit Red Wings	11	(1936–2008)
Boston Bruins	6	(1929–2011)
Chicago Blackhawks	6	(1934–2015)

The Montreal Canadiens are the oldest and, by far, the most successful National Hockey League team. In its earliest years, the Stanley Cup was awarded for different reasons, but since 1927, it has been given exclusively to the champion NHL team—and the Canadiens have won it roughly one year in every four. Their most successful years were the 1940s through the 1970s, when the team was inspired by all-time greats like Maurice Richard and Guy Lafleur.

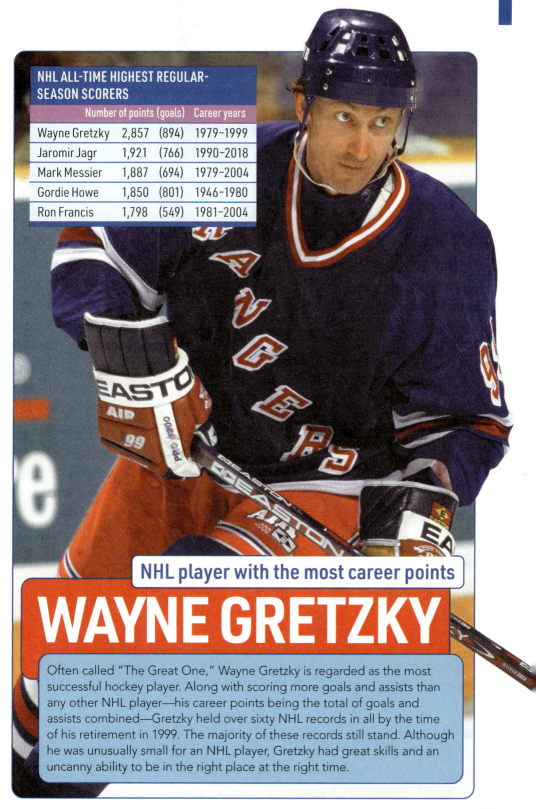

NHL ALL-TIME HIGHEST REGULAR-SEASON SCORERS			
	Number of points	(goals)	Career years
Wayne Gretzky	2,857	(894)	1979–1999
Jaromir Jagr	1,921	(766)	1990–2018
Mark Messier	1,887	(694)	1979–2004
Gordie Howe	1,850	(801)	1946–1980
Ron Francis	1,798	(549)	1981–2004

NHL player with the most career points

WAYNE GRETZKY

Often called "The Great One," Wayne Gretzky is regarded as the most successful hockey player. Along with scoring more goals and assists than any other NHL player—his career points being the total of goals and assists combined—Gretzky held over sixty NHL records in all by the time of his retirement in 1999. The majority of these records still stand. Although he was unusually small for an NHL player, Gretzky had great skills and an uncanny ability to be in the right place at the right time.

First woman to play in an NHL game

MANON RHÉAUME

Manon Rhéaume had a fine career as a goaltender in women's ice hockey, earning World Championship gold medals with the Canadian National Women's Team. She is also the first—and only—woman to play for an NHL club. On September 23, 1992, she played one period for the Tampa Bay Lightning in an exhibition game against the St. Louis Blues, during which she saved seven of nine shots. She later played twenty-four games for various men's teams in the professional International Hockey League.

The NASCAR drivers' championship has been contested since 1949. California native Jimmie Johnson is tied at the top of the all-time wins list with seven, but his five-season streak, 2006–2010, is easily the best in the sport's history. Johnson's racing career began on 50cc motorcycles when he was five years old. All of his NASCAR championship wins were achieved driving Chevrolets. He won eighty-three NASCAR races in his career, the last in 2017. He retired from NASCAR in 2020 but still competes in IndyCar events.

Most consecutive NASCAR championship wins

JIMMIE JOHNSON

NASCAR CHAMPIONSHIP WINS

Number of wins		Years in which the title was won
Jimmie Johnson	7	2006, 2007, 2008, 2009, 2010, 2013, 2016
Dale Earnhardt Sr.	7	1980, 1986, 1987, 1990, 1991, 1993, 1994
Richard Petty	7	1964, 1967, 1971, 1972, 1974, 1975, 1979
Jeff Gordon	4	1995, 1997, 1998, 2001

Most career wins in Formula One

LEWIS HAMILTON

In 2007, Lewis Hamilton—Formula One's first-ever Black driver—lined up in a McLaren at the 2007 Australian Grand Prix and finished third. He missed out on the title that year but won in 2008 to become F1's youngest champion. In 2013, he switched to a Mercedes, which seemed like a misstep, but the German manufacturer made the most of the sport's regulation changes, and Hamilton powered to consecutive titles in 2014 and 2015. He lost out to teammate Nico Rosberg in 2016 but rebounded with four straight titles between 2017 and 2020 to match Michael Schumacher's all-time mark of seven world titles. Heralded as one of F1's greatest ambassadors, by the end of the 2024 season, Hamilton holds the record for the most poles (104), podium finishes (202), and race wins (105).

MOST F1 CAREER VICTORIES

105	Lewis Hamilton (UK, 2007–present)
91	Michael Schumacher (Germany, 1991–2006, 2010–2012)
62	Max Verstappen (The Netherlands, 2015–present)
53	Sebastian Vettel (Germany, 2007–2022)
51	Alain Prost (France, 1980–1991, 1993)

Most successful surfer of all time

KELLY SLATER

Born on February 11, 1972, Kelly Slater grew up in Cocoa Beach, Florida, and started surfing at the age of five. By age ten, he was winning age-division events up and down the Atlantic coast, and in 1984, he won his first age-division national title. He turned professional in 1990, won his first pro event—the Rip Curl Pro in France—in 1992, and ended the year by becoming world champion for the first time. He claimed five successive world titles between 1994 and 1998 before taking a break from the sport—only to return in 2002 and earn another five titles between 2005 and 2011. His haul of eleven World Surf League titles is an all-time record.

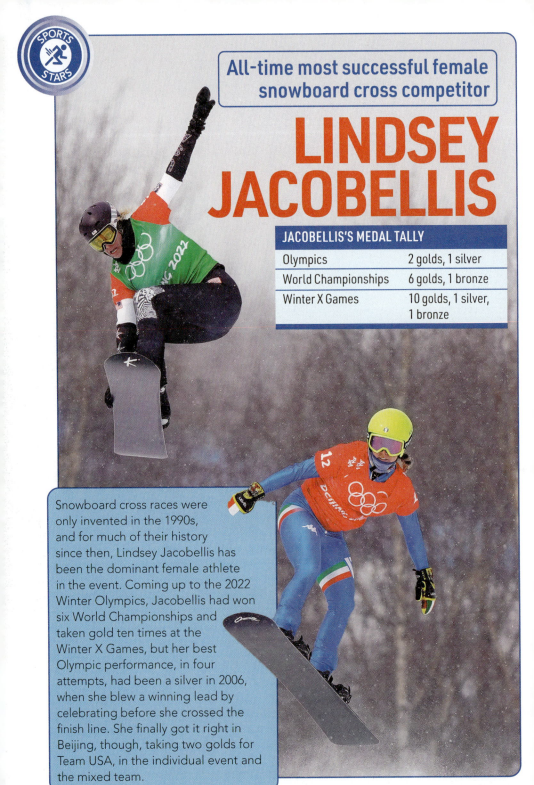

All-time most successful female snowboard cross competitor

LINDSEY JACOBELLIS

JACOBELLIS'S MEDAL TALLY	
Olympics	2 golds, 1 silver
World Championships	6 golds, 1 bronze
Winter X Games	10 golds, 1 silver, 1 bronze

Snowboard cross races were only invented in the 1990s, and for much of their history since then, Lindsey Jacobellis has been the dominant female athlete in the event. Coming up to the 2022 Winter Olympics, Jacobellis had won six World Championships and taken gold ten times at the Winter X Games, but her best Olympic performance, in four attempts, had been a silver in 2006, when she blew a winning lead by celebrating before she crossed the finish line. She finally got it right in Beijing, though, taking two golds for Team USA, in the individual event and the mixed team.

Highest pole vault ARMAND DUPLANTIS

Born in 1999 and raised in Louisiana by an American father and Swedish mother, Armand "Mondo" Duplantis started setting pole-vault records when he was still in elementary school. After choosing to compete for his mother's homeland, he landed his first big win in adult competition in the 2018 European Athletics Championships. In 2019, he gained a silver medal in the World Championships, but in 2022 he moved ahead of the field in his event, setting a new world record of 6.21 meters (20 feet, 4.25 inches). He has since gone on to break the record on five occasions, most recently with a leap of 6.26 meters (20 feet, 6.25 inches) in Chorzow, Poland, on August 25, 2024.

OLYMPICS
trending

AMERICA'S SWEETHEART ILONA MAHER INSPIRES A GENERATION

US rugby star Ilona Maher became one of the most iconic social media stars of the 2024 Olympics after she spoke out about comments calling her "too tall and muscular" to be attractive. Five foot ten and broad-shouldered, Maher is a two-time Olympian who now has both a bronze and a silver medal to her name. Maher has used her platform to empower girls to love their bodies and to inspire more girls to play rugby.

THE ULTIMATE CHEERLEADER SNOOP DOGG'S IMPECCABLE OLYMPIC COVERAGE

Some of the most memorable fashion from the 2024 Olympic Games came from rapper Snoop Dogg, who traveled to Paris as an Olympic correspondent. His eccentric and patriotic outfits included tailored equestrian clothing, star-spangled T-shirts, and a shirt emblazoned with the face of American Olympian Kelly Cheng. Snoop Dogg's enthusiasm for the events proved infectious and boosted NBC's viewership.

BIZARRE BREAKING RAYGUN'S KANGAROO POSE
BREAKS THE INTERNET Breakdancing was introduced to the Olympic Games in 2024, and the appearance of Australian dancer Raygun caused the Internet to go wild. Thirty-six-year-old Raygun (real name Rachael Gunn) broke out some bizarre moves in the women's B-girl competition, including kangaroo hopping and the sprinkler. Her amateur performance sparked viral jokes and memes that will forever be associated with Olympic breakdancing.

SKATING SENSATION THE
YOUNGEST OLYMPIAN At eleven years old, Zheng Haohao was the youngest athlete to take part in the Paris Summer Olympics. Representing China, Zheng took part in the skateboarding event, where she scored 63.19 points in the women's park preliminary contest but did not make it to the finals. Many articles commented on the age gap between her and the oldest skateboarder at the games, Britain's Andy Macdonald, who was fifty-one.

THE MUFFIN MAN NORWEGIAN OLYMPIAN'S
TASTY TIKTOKS The chocolate muffins in the Olympic Village propelled Norwegian swimmer Henrik Christiansen to fame in Paris, as the athlete gleefully posted TikToks about all the baked goods he was consuming. As a swimmer, Christiansen needs a massive daily calorie intake, and he seemed to relish earning some of those calories in the form of "choccy muffins"—rated 11/10 in his enthusiastic TikTok review.

PARIS 2024

Youngest medalist at the 2024 Summer Olympics

ARISA TREW

Born to a Japanese mother and a Welsh father, Australia's Arisa Trew took up skateboarding at the age of eight. She announced her arrival on the global stage on June 23, 2023, when she became the first female skateboarder in history to execute a successful 720 trick in a competition. The trick, which involves two full rotations in midair, was first made famous by the legendary Tony Hawk. More was to come the following year: On May 29, 2024, Trew became the first female skateboarder to land a 900 and then, on August 6, 2024, she recorded a score of 93.18 to land women's park skateboarding gold at the 2024 Olympic Games. At just fourteen years and eighty-six days, Trew became the Paris Games's youngest medalist.

KATIE LEDECKY

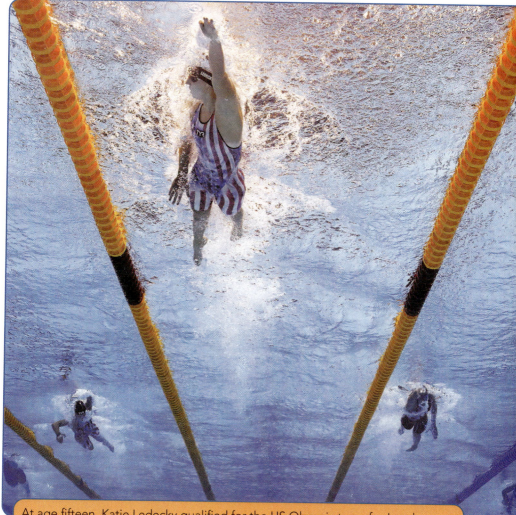

At age fifteen, Katie Ledecky qualified for the US Olympic team for London 2012 and surged to 800-meter freestyle gold. Further success followed at the 2013 World Championships when she took four gold medals, setting the 800m and 1500m world records in the process, and she raced to five more World Championship golds in 2015. She took four gold medals at the 2016 Olympics and five golds at the 2017 World Championships. The gold rush continued with two more medals at the 2020 Olympics, four at the 2022 World Championships, two at the 2023 World Championships, and two at the 2024 Olympics. With thirty Olympic and World Championship gold medals, plus 11 gold medals from other competitions, she is the most decorated female swimmer in history.

Most Olympic golds won by an individual

MICHAEL PHELPS

Michael Phelps may be the greatest competitive swimmer ever. He did not win any medals at his first Olympics in 2000, but at each of the Summer Games from 2004 through 2016, he was the most successful individual athlete of any nation. When he announced his retirement after London 2012, he was already the most decorated Olympic athlete ever—but he didn't stay retired for long. At Rio 2016, he won five more golds and a silver, taking his medal total to twenty-eight—twenty-three of them gold.

MOST SUCCESSFUL OLYMPIANS
Number of medals won (gold)

Michael Phelps, USA	Swimming	2004–2016	28 (23)
Larisa Latynina, USSR	Gymnastics	1956–1964	18 (9)
Marit Bjørgen, Norway	Cross-country skiing	2002–2018	15 (8)
Nikolai Andrianov, USSR	Gymnastics	1972–1980	15 (7)

SIMONE BILES

Most decorated gymnast ever

Simone Biles won her first three World Championship medals in 2013 at the age of sixteen and has added to her total every season since then, apart from a career break in 2017. Biles is only 4 feet, 8 inches tall, but her tiny frame is full of power and grace, displayed most memorably in her favorite event, floor exercise. She is so good that several special moves are named after her—and they are so difficult that she is the only competitor so far to perform these in championships. To date, she has won seven Olympic and twenty-three World Championship gold medals. Biles has also been widely praised as a champion for mental health awareness and for her bravery in speaking out as a victim in an abuse scandal in her sport.

World record holder in women's 400-meter hurdles

SYDNEY MCLAUGHLIN-LEVRONE

Sydney McLaughlin-Levrone triumphed at the 2021 Tokyo Olympics in perhaps the greatest track race of the Games. McLaughlin-Levrone had set a new world record of 51.90 seconds in the US Olympic trials, edging ahead of her great rival, Dalilah Muhammad. Muhammad smashed that mark with 51.58 in the Tokyo final, but McLaughlin-Levrone stayed in front with an astonishing 51.46 win. She has since gone on to break her own record on four occasions, most recently at the Olympic final at Paris in 2024, when she clocked 50.37 seconds.

FASTEST WOMEN'S 400M HURDLES		
Time in seconds		
Sydney McLaughlin-Levrone (USA) 50.37		2024
Sydney McLaughlin-Levrone (USA) 50.65		2024
Sydney McLaughlin (USA)	50.68	2022
Sydney McLaughlin (USA)	51.41	2022
Sydney McLaughlin (USA)	51.46	2021

Fastest man in the world
USAIN BOLT

FASTEST 100M SPRINTS OF ALL TIME
Time in seconds

Usain Bolt (Jamaica)	9.58	Berlin 2009
Usain Bolt (Jamaica)	9.63	London 2012
Usain Bolt (Jamaica)	9.69	Beijing 2008
Tyson Gay (USA)	9.69	Shanghai 2009
Yohan Blake (Jamaica)	9.69	Lausanne 2012

Jamaica's top athlete, Usain Bolt, is the greatest track sprinter who has ever lived. Other brilliant Olympic finalists have described how all they can do is watch as Bolt almost disappears into the distance. Usain's greatest victories have been his triple Olympic gold medals at London 2012 and Rio 2016, plus two gold medals from Beijing 2008. Usain also holds the 100-meter world record (9.58s) and the 200-meter record (19.19s), both from the 2009 World Championships.

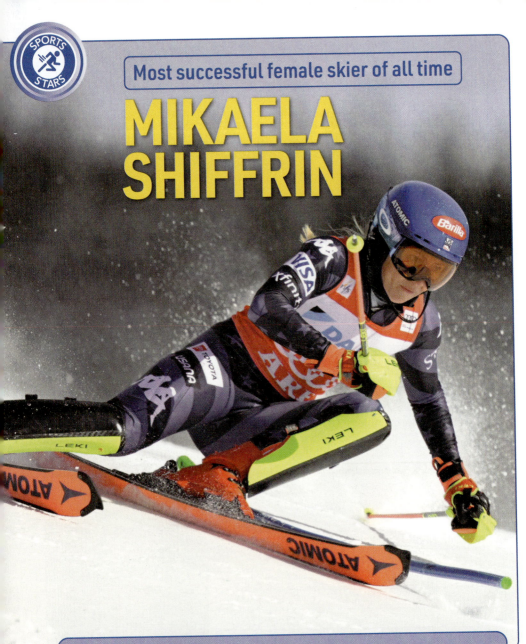

Most successful female skier of all time

MIKAELA SHIFFRIN

USA's Mikaela Shiffrin made her World Cup debut at age fifteen in 2011. Three years later, she took gold in slalom at the 2014 Winter Olympics in Sochi to become the youngest-ever champion. She was World Cup slalom champion again in 2014 and 2015, became overall champion for the first time in 2017, won a second Winter Olympic gold medal at Pyeonchang, South Korea, in 2018, and by year's end, she had become the first skier in history to have won a World Cup race in all six individual ski disciplines. On March 11, 2023, she notched her eighty-seventh win to pass Ingemar Stenmark's record of eighty-six wins to become the most successful alpine skier in history. With ninety-seven wins to her name, Shiffrin may hold that title for some time.

Erin Jackson gained her first big sporting successes as an in-line speed skater and in roller derby. Jackson was an in-line-skating medalist in the 2015 Pan-American Games, and it was only in 2016 that she switched to speed skating on ice. She lacked experience at her first Olympics in 2018 but did everything right in Beijing in 2022. Her winning time of 37.04 seconds in the 500-meter race gave her a 0.08-second margin of victory. There are two types of indoor ice-skating races. Long-track races in international competitions take place on a 400-meter circuit, similar in size to a standard running track. Short-track races take place on a circuit created on an international-size hockey rink. The long-track races are faster, but the short-track ones can be very dramatic, with many crashes and falls.

First Black woman to win an individual Winter Olympic gold medal

ERIN JACKSON

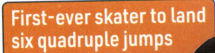

First-ever skater to land six quadruple jumps

NATHAN CHEN

Nathan Chen made skating history at the 2018 Winter Olympics by being the first-ever skater to attempt and land six quadruple jumps during one performance. Quad jumps—in which the skater spins around four times while in the air—are among the hardest moves in skating, and grouping several of them in one program makes them more difficult still. Chen's record-breaking moves did not win a medal, because he skated poorly in another part of the competition, but he won the 2018 World Championship after landing his six quads once again. He retained his title in 2019 and added a third world gold in 2021. Chen finally won Olympic gold at Beijing in 2022 in the men's singles competition, though this time attempting "only" five quad jumps in his free skate program.

SHAUN WHITE

A professional skateboarder, successful musician, and Olympic and X Games star, Shaun White has an astonishing range of talents. He has won more X Games gold medals than anyone else, but his three Olympic golds, in the half-pipe competitions in 2006, 2010, and 2018, the most ever by a snowboarder, are perhaps his biggest achievement. The best of all was in 2018, when he landed two super-difficult back-to-back tricks in the final round to jump into first place. White's medal happened to be the 100th for the US at the Winter Olympics. White again made the US Olympic team for Beijing 2022, just missing out on another medal with fourth place in the half-pipe. He announced his retirement from competition after this event.

Most decorated Paralympian ever

TRISCHA ZORN

Trischa Zorn is the most successful Paralympian of all time, having won an astonishing fifty-five medals, forty-one of them gold, at the Paralympic Games from 1980 to 2004. She won every Paralympic event she entered from 1980 to 1988. Zorn is blind and helps military veterans with disabilities enter the world of parasport. Zorn was inducted into the Paralympic Hall of Fame in 2012.

LEADING PARALYMPIC MEDALISTS
Number of medals won

Trischa Zorn, USA	55
Heinz Frei, Switzerland	35
Jonas Jacobsson, Sweden	30
Zipora Rubin-Rosenbaum, Israel	30
Jessica Long, USA	29

Country with the most all-time Paralympic medals

USA

COUNTRIES WITH THE MOST PARALYMPIC MEDALS

Total number of medals won	
United States	2,723
Great Britain	2,078
Germany*	1,979
China	1,519
France	1,350

*Includes totals of former East and West Germany

Although China topped the Paralympic medal table at the 2024 Summer Games in Paris (220 medals), with the United States coming in third (105), the United States comfortably leads the all-time medal count in the Paralympic Summer Games. Norway heads the standings in the Winter Games, with the United States in second place, giving the United States an overall medal total that will be unbeatable for many years to come.

A

Abdul-Jabbar, Kareem 244
Abu Dhabi 58
Abu Dhabi Autonomous
  Racing League (A2RL) 46
Abyssinian cat 152
Academy Awards 33, 34, 35
Actors 37
Actresses 33, 34, 36, 43
Africa 168, 170
African bush elephant 114
African ostrich egg 135
AI-driven cars 46
Aircraft 47, 54, 145, 232
Airspeed 141
AirVenture 232
Alabama 184
Alaska 185
Alaska Airlines 47
Albertsons Stadium 195
Albums 9
Aldabra Atoll 150
Alerce Milenario 158
Aleut 185
All-Star Game 237
Alligators 192
AlNassr 86
Amazon River 170
Amazon River basin 132
American Football 7, 245–7
American Revolutionary War
  (1775–1783) 191, 203
America's Dead Sea 227
America's Got Talent 288
Amphitheaters 188
Amur tiger 119
Ancient Earth 157
Anderson, Wes 24, 36
Andrianov, Nikolai 268
Angora rabbit 146
Anguiano, Susanne and Benny
  144
Animals 108–53, 189, 192, 196
Animation 26, 30, 39
Anoka 206
ANS Global 74
ANS Living Wall System 74
Antarctica 136, 164
Ants 140
Apex 110
Apollo 10 56–7
Apollo 11 56
Apple 88
Apps 88, 98

Arabian Desert 168
Arden House 216
Argentina 251, 253
Arizona 186
Arkansas 187
ARP 142 84
Art Basel Miami Beach 183
Artwork 183
Asheville 216
Asian elephant 114
Asian giant hornet 139
Astronauts 47, 85
AstroTurf 195
Athletics 270–1
Auld-Thomas, Luke 62
Australia 70, 111, 123, 130, 167
Australian Grand Prix 260
Australian Open 254, 255
Aviation 232
Azerbaijan 169

B

"Baby Dev" 288
"Baby Shark Dance" 89
Bacteria 233
Bad Bunny 20
Bad to the Bone 48
Bald eagle 134
Bale, Christian 36
Ballet 207
Ballon d'Or 253
Baltimore 63
Baltimore Ravens 7
Bananas 183
Bangladesh 178, 179
BANGTANTV 31
Banks 229
Barbie (doll) 237
Barbie (film) 35, 36
Barcelona 253
Bark Air 145
BASE jumping 231, 240
Baseball 197, 236, 248
Basketball 237, 241, 242–4
Batagaika Crater 174
Bats 115
Battle of the Little Bighorn
  (1876) 224
Beagle 149
Beasts of the Southern Wild 34
the Beatles 11, 14, 188
Becky G 13
Bees 139, 217
Bell, Chanell 145

Bell, John 198
Beluga caviar 169
Beluga sturgeon 169
Beyoncé 7, 19
Bieber, Justin 10
Big Ten Conference 247
Big Way 231
Biles, Simone 269
Billboard charts 6, 7, 8, 11,
  12, 20
Billboard Music Awards
  (BBMAs) 13, 21
Biltmore Estate 216
Biltmore House 216
Biofuel 84
Birds 111, 132–7
"Birds of a Feather" (Billie
  Eilish) 8
Bison 111, 199
Bjørgen, Marit 268
Black people 229
Black Rock Desert 52
Blackburn, Abner 182
BLACKPINK 7, 31
Blake, Yohan 271
Bleymaier, Gene 195
Block Blast! 88
Blokhus Sculpture Park 79
Bloodhound 52
"The Blue" 195
Blue whale 125, 126
Blueberries 182
Blueberry barrens 182
BMX 240
Boeing 47
Boise State 236
Bolt, Usain 271
Bollywood 31
Bonner, DeWanna 243
Bonnie 144
Boone, Benson 8
Bordeaux 73
Boston Breakers 250
Boston Bruins 256
Boston Red Sox 248
Botswana 157
Bowie, David 11
Brady, Tom 246
Brat green 62
Brazil 251
Breakdancing 265
Bridge Day 231
Bridges 63, 72, 201, 231
Bristlecone pine 158

Bristol 222
British Shorthair cat 152
Broadway 40–1, 42
Brookesia nana 131
Brooks, Garth 14
Brown, Barnum 209
Bryan, Zach 21
Bryant, Kobe 244
BTS 7, 15
Bugatti La Voiture Noire 49
Bulldogs 149
Bureau of Land Management (BLM) 211
Burj Khalifa 68–9
Buses 48

C

Cafés 63
"Caitlin Clark Effect" 237
California 158, 159, 172, 177, 183, 188
California redwood 159
Call of Duty: Black Ops 6 99
Call of Duty: Modern Warfare 3 99
Call of Duty: Warzone Mobile 88
Cambridge Medical Robotics 105
Camp Nou 65
Canada 153, 172
Canadian National Women's Team 258
Candy 190
Canyons 164
Cape Canaveral 57
Capitol buildings 203
Carey, Mariah 17
Cargo ships 63
Carolina Reaper 223
Carpenter, Sabrina 6, 8
Cars 46, 49, 52, 259–60
Carter, Blue Ivy 7
Carvings 224
Caspian Sea 169
Castles 66–7
Cat Fanciers' Association 152
Catchings, Tamika 243
Category 6 waterpark 50
Cathedrals 62
Cats
  domestic cats 95, 144, 152–3
  wild cats 118–19, 226
Cattelan, Maurizio 183
Caves 162–3

Caviar 169
Cena, John 26
Central Plaza 64
Chameleon 131
Charles, James 92
Charles, Tina 243
Charli XCX 62
Charlie Brown (spacecraft) 56
Chattanooga Bakery 225
Cheetah 118
Chen, Nathan 274
Cheng, Kelly 264
Chernow, Ron 42
Chicago Blackhawks 256
Chicago White Sox 236
Chihuahua 151
China 53, 64, 72, 76–7, 201, 277
Chomolungma 166
Christiansen, Henrik 265
Chu, Dr. Betty 146
Churches 215
Cincinnati Red Stockings 197
Cincinnati Zoo 118
Cinnamon rolls 220
Cities 73
Citystars 71
Clark, Caitlin 237, 242
Climate change 167, 174, 176
Coast Douglas-fir 159
Coast redwood 159
Coastal Carolina Chanticleers 195
CoComelon 30
College football 99
Colman, Olivia 27
Colorado 177, 189
Colugo 113
Computer games 85, 88, 98, 99, 100–3
Comstock Lode 182
Connecticut 190
Connor, Kit 27
Continental Congress 203
Coober Pedy 70
Cookies 225
Copenhagen 73
Coprolites 186
Coral reefs 167
Corn 210
Coronal mass ejection 156
Country music 18, 19
Country Music Awards 18
COVID-19 79
Cowboy Carter (Beyoncé) 7, 19

CR Fuxing 53
CR Harmony 53
Crater of Diamonds State Park 187
Craters 174
Crayola 221
Crayons 221
Crazy Horse Memorial 224
Cripps, Donald 231
Crocodiles 130, 192
Cross Island Chapel 215
Cruise ships 50, 80
Crystal Lagoons 71
Cullinan diamond 157
Currie, Smokin' Ed 223
Curtiss-Wright Field 232
Custer, General 224
Cycling 240
Cyrus, Billy Ray 17
Cyrus, Miley 19

D

Dachshund 149
Daga, Arnav 78
Dahl, Roald 43
Dali 63
D'Amelio, Charli 93
Dance, Thomas 203
Danyang-Kunshan Grand Bridge 72
Davis, Viola 36
Deadpool & Wolverine 32, 38
"Defying Gravity" (*Wicked*) 25
Delaware 191
Demetriou, Cleo 43
Denman Glacier 164
Denmark 73, 79
Denver Nuggets 244
Desert locust 141
Deserts 168
"Despacito" (Luis Fonsi) 10, 17, 89
Despicable Me 39
Detroit Red Wings 256
Detroit Tigers 236
Devon Rex 152
Diamante 71
Diamonds 157, 187
DiCaprio, Leonardo 36
DiMaggio, Joe 248
Diners 213
Dinosaurs 110, 125, 157, 209
Diseases 142
Disney 32, 38, 41, 66

Djokovic, Novac 255
Dogs 94, 144–5, 148–9, 151
Dolls 237
Donkey 145
Doug the Pug 94
Draco 113
Dracula ant 140
Dragon Ball: Sparking Zero 99
Dragonfly 143
Dragons 106–7, 128
Drake 12, 21
Dream Cruises Management Ltd 80
Dubai 64
Dubuque, Iowa 198
Dude Perfect 241
Dune 85
Duplantis, Armand "Mondo" 263

E

EA Sports College Football 25 99
EAA Aviation Museum 232
Eagle, bald 134
Eagles (band) 14
Earnhardt, Dale Sr. 259
Earth, incredible 154–79
East Newark 213
Easton 221
Eggs 135, 136
Egypt 71, 81
Eilish, Billie 8, 35
El Tatio 165
El Último Tour del Mundo (Bad Bunny) 20
Elephant 114
Elk 189
Emmy Awards 27
Emoji 104
Emperor penguin 136–7
Enchiladas 214
Environmental Transport Association (ETA) 51
Epaulette shark 123
Eras Tour (Taylor Swift) 6, 16
Erivo, Cynthia 25
"Espresso" (Sabrina Carpenter) 6, 8
Estrada, Roberto 214
Etruscan shrew 115
Eucalyptus trees 112
European Athletics Championships 263
Everest, Mount 166
Everest, Sir George 166
Everglades National Park 192
Everything Everywhere All at Once 33

Exotic cat 152
Experimental Aircraft Association 232
Extreme sports 238
Eyak 185

F

FACE (Jimin) 15
Factories 218, 221
Fairs 202
Fairy-Tale Castle 66
Falabella horse 147
Fall, Albert 230
Fanny 106–7
Fayetteville 231
Feathers 133
Federer, Roger 255
Fenelon Place Elevator 198
Ferrari World 58
Ferrera, America 36
Fett, Boba 24
FIFA World Cup 86, 250, 251–2
Fire-bellied snake 129
Firefly 84
Fires 172–3
Fireworks 200
First National Bank Stadium 65
Fish 113, 126–7, 169
Flint Hills 199
Florida 192
FloyyMenor 8
Flying fish 113
Flying lemur 113
Flying lizard 113
Flying squid 113
Flying squirrel 113
Fonsi, Luis 10, 17, 89
Football 7, 245–7
Football fields 195
Forbes 16, 36, 37, 91
Forest Citys 197
Formula One 260
Formula Rossa 58
Fossils 110, 186, 209
Fourth of July 222
Fox 26
France 62, 251, 277
Franchesca (rabbit) 146
Francis, Ron 257
Francis Scott Key Bridge 63
Frandsen, George 186
Fred (donkey) 145
Frei, Heinz 276
French bulldog (Frenchie) 149
French Open 254, 255
Frog 129
Fruit 160, 182, 183
Fuel 84
Fuerza Regida 13

G

G-force 58
Gaga, Lady 8
Galápagos penguin 137
Galaxies 84
Gaming 85, 88, 98, 99, 100–3
Garden of Edam 162
Gas leaks 145
Gas stations 230
Gay, Tyson 271
General Earth Minerals 187
Gentoo penguin 137
Georgia 193
German shepherd dog 149
German shorthaired pointer 149
Germany 66, 251, 252, 277
Gerwig, Greta 36
Geysers 165
Giant Amazon water lily 161
Giant sequoia 159
Gienger, Travis 160, 206
Gillis, Sarah 47
Giraffe 120–1
Glaciers 164
Global Destination Sustainability Movement 73
Global warming 157
Globe skimmer 143
Golden Globes 34
Golden poison dart frog 129
Golden retriever 149
Goliath bird-eating tarantula 138
Gopalganj 178
Gordon, Jeff 259
Gorilla 116
Gosling, Ryan 36
Goth athlete 236
Grammy Awards 6, 7, 8, 19, 21, 35
Gran Abuelo 158
Grand Prismatic Spring 233
Grand Slams 254, 255
Grande, Ariana 25
Graves, J. K. 198
Gray, Conner and Owen 96
Great Barrier Reef 123, 167
Great Britain 277
Great Lakes 205
Great Salt Lake 227
Great Sphinx 81
Great Victoria Desert 168
Great Wall of China 238
Great Wall of Vietnam 162
Great white shark 127
Green walls 74
Gretzky, Wayne "The Great One" 257

Ground speed 141
Grupo Frontera 13
Guinness World Records 95, 96, 102–3, 145, 186, 223
Gulf of Mexico 226
Gymnastics 269

H

Haas, Eduard III 190
Hailstones 178, 183
Hale, Sarah Josepha 204
Halloween 206
Halton, Leah 92
Hamilton 42
Hamilton, Alexander 42
Hamilton, Lewis 260
Hamm, Mia 250
Hamwi, Ernest 208
Hang Son Doong 162–3
Hanks, Tom 26
Happy Madison Productions 37
Harding, Warren G. 230
Harrison, George 11
Harry Potter 32, 92
Hawaii 194
Hawk, Tony 266
Hayd, Nora 236
Heartstopper 27
Heat waves 176
Hell Creek Formation 209
Helldivers 2 99
Helsinki 73
High tech 82–107
Hill, Cypress 25
Hillary, Sir Edmund 166
Himalayas 166
Hoatzin 132
Hoffman, Mat "The Condor" 240
Hollywood Bowl Orchestra 188
Honey 217
Honeybees 139, 217
Hong Kong 64
Hornets 139
Horsefly 141
Horses 147, 211
Hot springs 233
Hot Topic 236
Hottest month 176
Houston Texans 7
Houston, Whitney 11
How Ridiculous 241
Howe, Gordie 257
Howler monkey 122
Hubble Space Telescope 75
Huddleston, John Wesley 187
Hungarian sheepdog 148
Hungry Studio 88
Hunt, Richard Morris 216

Hurdles 270
Hveravellir 165
Hybe Labels 31
Hyperion 159

I

Ibrahimović, Zlatan 249
ICE 3 53
Ice-cream cones 208
Ice hockey 256–8
Ice-skating 273–4
Icon of the Seas 50
Idaho 195
If You're Reading This It's Too Late 12
Iger, Bob 38
Illinois 196
India 78, 130, 178, 179
Indiana 197, 210
Indiana Fever 237, 242
Indonesia 123, 128
IndyCar 259
Ingram, Kerry 43
Insects 139–43, 217
Inside Out 2 29, 38
Instagram 86, 94–5
Inter Miami 253
International Commerce Centre (ICC) 64
International Finance Centre 64
International Hockey League 258
International Space Station (ISS) 47
Inuit 185
Iolani Palace 194
Iowa 198
Iowa Hawkeyes 237, 242
iPhone 88
Iran 169
Isaacman, Jared 47
Italy 251
iTunes 12

J

Jackman, Hugh 38
Jackson, Erin 273
Jackson, Mississippi 207
Jacobellis, Lindsey 262
Jacobsson, Jonas 276
Jagr, Jaromir 257
Jaguar 119
James Bond 32, 35
James, LeBron 244
James Webb Space Telescope 75, 84
Japan 63, 85, 252
Jasper 172

Jay-Z 16, 19
Jet fuel 84
Jiaozhou Bay Bridge 201
Jim Crow laws 229
Jimin 15
Joannitante 85
Johansson, Scarlett 36
John Hopkins University 55
Johnson, Jimmie 259
Jonathan (tortoise) 150
Jones, Bobby 193
Jones, Olga 144
Jordan, Michael 244
Jungkook 15

K

K-pop 7, 15
K2 166
Kagera River 170
Kaji, Ryan 91
Kalahari Desert 168
Kalakaua, King 194
Kanchenjunga 166
Kansas 199
Kansas City Chiefs 28
Kanyaboyina, Sudhakar 46
Karowe diamond mine 157
Kazakhstan 169
Kekiongas 197
Kelce, Travis 28
Kentucky 200
Kentucky Derby 200
Kenya 170
Khafre 81
Khalifa Avenue 74
Khasi Hills 179
Kiely, Sophia 43
King, Zach 92
King penguin 111, 137
Kirishima Shuzo 63
Kitti's hog-nosed bat 115
Koala 112
Kobe (dog) 145
Kolkata 78
Komodo dragon 128
Komondor 148
Kyoto 85

L

La Liga goals 253
LA wildfires 172–3
Labrador retriever 149
Lady Gaga 8
Lafleur, Guy 256
Lake Huron 169
Lake Michigan 169
Lake Pontchartrain Causeway 201
Lake Superior 169

Lake Victoria 169, 170
Lakes 169, 227
Lakota tribe 111, 224
Las Brisas 71
Las Cruces 214
Las Vegas Strip 241
Latynina, Larisa 268
Laurence Olivier Awards 43
Leaves 161
Lebo M 41
Led Zeppelin 14
Ledecky, Katie 267
LEGO 80
Lemurs 113
Lennon, John 11
Lent 184
Leopard 119
Leopardus pardalis albescens 226
Leroux, Gaston 40
Lhotse 166
Lidar surveys 62
Lighthouses 205
Lightning 175
Lil Nas X 17
Liliuokalani, Queen 194
Lilly, Kristine 250
Lincoln, Abraham 204
Lincoln Park Zoo 196
Lion 118, 119
Lion King, The 41
Lisa 7
Lizards 113, 128
Lloud 7
Lloyd, Carli 250
Locusts 141
London Symphony Orchestra 25
Long, Jessica 276
Los Angeles 172–3, 238
Los Angeles County 183
Los Angeles FC 249
Los Angeles Hollywood Bowl 188
Los Angeles Philharmonic 188
Louisiana 201
Ludwig II, King of Bavaria 66

M
Macaroni penguin 137
Macdonald, Andy 265
Mach 9.6 54
McLaren 260
McLaughlin-Levrone, Sydney 270
Madagascar 131
Maezawa, Yusaku 87
Maglev train 53
Magnetic storm 156
MahaSamutr 71

Maher, Ilona 264
Maine 182, 202
Maine Coon Cat 152
Makalu 166
Malaria 142
Malaysia 130
Malbork Castle 67
Malone, Karl 244
Mandrill 117
Maple syrup 228
Mardi Gras 184
Mariana Trench 164
Mario 101
Mario Kart 101
Martinez, Josef 249
Marvel Cinematic Universe 32
Maryland 203
Maryland State House 203
Massachusetts 204
Math 288
Matilda 43
Mattel 237
Maverick 206
Mawsynram 179
Maya 62
Medford 220
Megaflash 175
Melbourne Ground 65
Mercedes 260
Mesoamerican Barrier Reef 167
Messi, Lionel 86, 253
Messier, Mark 257
Methuselah (tree) 158
Michigan 205
Michigan Stadium 65
Michigan Wolverines 247
Microsoft 102
Middlesex County Museum 213
Milwaukee 232
Minecraft 102–3
Minefaire 2016 102–3
Mining 182
Minitrailer 51
Minnesota 206
Miracle Milly (Chihuahua) 151
Miranda, Lin-Manuel 42
Mississippi 207
Mississippi-Missouri river system 170
Missouri 208
MrBeast 31, 90
Mitchell, Earl Sr. 225
The Mitchells vs. the Machines 94
MLS (Major League Soccer) 249
Mobile 184

Mobility scooters 51
Monkeys 117, 122
Monopoly Go! 88
Monster school bus 48
Montana 209
Montana, Joe 245
Montreal Canadiens 256
Moon 56, 156
MoonPies 225
Moradabad 178
Mosquito 142
Moss, Randy 245
Mount Everest 166
Mount Rushmore 224
Mount Shasta 177
Mountain ash 159
Mountains 166, 224
Movies 25, 29, 32, 33, 34, 38–9
MTV Video Music Awards (VMAs) 7
Muhammad, Dalilah 270
Museum of the Rockies 209
Museums 46, 186, 193, 194, 209, 213, 230, 232
Music 4–21, 31, 89
Musicals 25, 40–3
Myanmar 115
Mystrium camillae 140

N
Nadal, Rafael 255
Nakheel Landscapes 74
Nala Cat 95
Nano-chameleon 131
Nansen Ski Club 212
Narwhal 124
NASA 47, 54, 55, 56, 75, 85, 156
NASCAR 225, 259
National Association baseball 197
National League 248
National Oceanic and Atmospheric Administration (NOAA) 176
National parks 111, 144, 165, 189, 192, 199
Native Americans 111, 185, 204
Nazaré 171
NBA (National Basketball Association) 237, 244
NBC 264
NCAA 237, 242, 243
Nebraska 210
Nepal 166
Nests 134
Netflix 7, 27, 37
Netherlands 252
Neuschwanstein Castle 66
Nevada 182, 211

Nevada Wild Horse Range 211
New Caledonia Barrier Reef 167
New England Patriots 246
New Hampshire 212
New Jersey 213
New Mexico 214
New River 231
New River Gorge Bridge 231
New York 215
New York City 64
New York Liberty 242
New York Mets 236
New York Yankees 248
NFL (National Football League) 7, 245–6
NHL (National Hockey League) 256–8
Nickelodeon 89
Nielsen, Per Ishøy 96
Nile River 170
Ningaloo Reef 167
Nintendo 98, 100, 101
Nintendo Museum 85
"No Time to Die" (Billie Eilish) 35
Nock, Freddy 239
Norgay, Tenzing 166
North Carolina 216
North Dakota 217
North Korea 65
Northern Lights 156
Norway 252
Notre-Dame 62

O

Oakland Athletics 248
O'Brien, Conan 26
Ocelot 226
O'Connell, Finneas 35
Oheka Castle 216
Ohio 218
Ohio State Buckeyes 247
Oil wells 219
Oklahoma 219
Oklahoma City Oil Field 219
Oklahoma State Capitol 219
Old Faithful 165
"Old Town Road" (Lil Nas X) 17
Olympic Games 212, 243, 250, 255, 264–75
The One 216
Oneida 215
Opal 70
Orakei Korako 165
Orange, Connecticut 190
Orangutan 111
Oregon 220
Oregon Ducks 247

Orinoco River basin 132
Oscars 33, 34, 35
Oseman, Alice 27
Oshkosh 232
Ostrich 118, 135
Owens, Terrell 245

P

Pac-12 Conference 247
Pagani Zonda HP Barchetta 49
Pajitnov, Alexey 98
Palaces 194
Pan-American Games 273
Papua New Guinea 123, 133
Paralympic Games 276–7
Paris 62, 264, 265, 266, 270, 277
Paris Saint-Germain 253
Parker Solar Probe 55
Pear Blossom Festival 220
Pearce, Christie 250
Pee 85
Pelé 251
the Penguin and the Egg 84
Penguins 111, 136–7
Pennsylvania 221
Pepper X 223
Peppers 223
Permafrost craters 174
Persian cat 152
Persson, Markus 102
Perutzki, Katharina 145
Pesto 111
Petit, Philippe 239
Petty, Richard 259
Petunia #1 219
PEZ candy 190
Phantom of the Opera, The 40
Phelps, Michael 268
Philadelphia Zoo 196
Phoenix Mercury 243
Pilgrims 204
Pinkfong 89
Pitt, Brad 36
Pixar 29
Planes 47, 54, 145, 232
Plants 161
Playing card structure 78
PlayStation 100
Plymouth, Massachusetts 204
Poison dart frog 129
Pokémon cards 96–7
Poland 67
Pole vaulting 263
Pons, Lily 188
Poo 84, 186
Poodle 149
Poozeum 186
Popcorn 210
Portugal 171

Prehn, Jens Ishøy 96
Presley, Elvis 14
Primates 116–17
Prince 11
Private houses 216
Pronghorn 118
Prost, Alain 260
Prune (cat) 153
PS2 100
Pumpkin 160, 206

Q

Qatar 74
Qin Shi Huang 76–7
Qogir 166
QTvan 51

R

Ra 81
Rabbit 146
Races 46
Ragdoll 152
Railroads 198
Rainfall 179
Rainforests 162
Rakus 111
Rap artists 12
Rapinoe, Megan 252
Raygun (Rachael Gunn) 265
Rayne Beau 144
Real Sociedad 249
Redwood National and State Parks 159
Reptiles 130–1
Reynolds, Ryan 38
Rhéaume, Manon 258
Rhode Island 222
Ribbon-tailed astrapia 133
Rice, Jerry 245
Richard, Maurice 256
Rihanna 16
Rip Curl Pro 261
Rivers 170
Roan, Chappell 7
Robbie, Margot 36
Roberto's Mexican Restaurant 214
Robinson, Jackie 193
Roblox 88
Robots 105–7
Rock Hill 223
Rocket Mortgage Field House 237
Rocky Mountain National Park 189
Roller coasters 58
Rolls-Royce Rose Noire Droptail 49
Romulus (donkey) 145

Ronaldo, Cristiano 86, 90
Rosberg, Nico 260
Rose Bowl 65, 247
Rottweiler 149
Royal Albert Hall 25
Royal Caribbean 50
Royal palaces 194
Rubin-Rosenbaum, Zipora 276
Rugby 264
Rungrado 1st of May Stadium 65
Running 271
Rushmore, Mount 224
Russia 169
Russian Blue cat 152
Ruth, Babe 248
Ruti 81
Ryan's World 91

S

Sagarmatha 166
Sahara Desert 168
St. Helena 150
St. Louis Blues 258
St. Louis Cardinals 248
St. Louis World's Fair 208
St. Luke Penny Savings Bank 229
Saltwater crocodile 130
Saltwater lakes 227
San Alfonso del Mar 71
San Francisco 110
San Francisco 49ers 28, 245
Sandcastles 79
Sandler, Adam 37
School bus 48
Schumacher, Michael 260
Science Museum 56
Scorsese, Martin 36
Scoville heat units (SHU) 223
Sculpture 81, 224
Sea Life Melbourne Aquarium 111
Sea lions 110
Segama River 130
Self-medication 111
Seychelles 150
Shaheed Minar 78
Shakira 13
Shanghai Maglev 53
Sharks 123, 126–7
Sharm El Sheikh 71
Shenzhen 64
Shiffrin, Mikaela 272
Ships 50, 63, 80
Shrews 115
Siberia 174
Siberian cat 152
Siberian tiger 119

Silver Lake 177
Simba 144
The Simpsons 25, 26
Sinclair, Christine 250
Singapore 73
Sitka spruce 159
Six Flags Hurricane Harbor Chicago 59
Skateboarding 238, 265, 266
Skating 273–4
Skiing 212, 272
Skowhegan State Fair 202
Skyscrapers 64, 68–9
Slater, Kelly 261
Slebir, Alo 171
Sleeping Beauty 66
Smith, Emmitt 245
Snakes 129
Snoop Dogg 264
Snoopy (spacecraft) 56
Snow leopard 119
Snowboarding 262, 275
Snowfall 177
Soccer 65, 86, 90, 249–53
Solar eclipse 156
Solar storms 156
Somerset Central Agricultural Society 202
Songs 8
Sony 100
Sotheby's 110, 183
South Carolina 223
South Carolina Gamecocks 237
South Dakota 224
Space 47, 55–7, 75, 84
Space telescopes 75, 84
Spacecraft 47, 55–7
Space suits 85
Space walks 47, 85
SpaceX Polaris Dawn 47
Spain 252
Speed skating 273
Sphynx 152, 153
Spider-Man 32
Spiders 138
Sports 193, 195, 197, 200, 234–77
Sports Hall of Fame 193
Sports Illustrated 99
Spotify 8, 9, 15, 20
Springbok 118
Sprinting 271
Squid 113
Squirrel, flying 113
Stadiums 65
Stage & screen 22–43
Stalagmites 162
Stanley Cup 256
Star Wars 24, 32

Starbucks 63
State capitols 219
State fairs 202
State stats 180–233
Stegosaurus 110
Stenmark, Ingemar 272
Steudtner, Sebastian 171
Stijger, Wilfred 79
Stockholm 73
Storms 156
Stratosphere (STRAT Tower) 241
Sudha Cars Museum 46
Sun 55, 156
Super Bowl 28, 94, 245, 246
Super Mario World 101
Super structures 60–81
Supersonic cars 52
Surfing 261
Surgical robots 105
Sustainable aviation fuel (SAF) 84
Sustainable cities 73
Swift, Taylor 6, 9, 11, 16, 21, 28
Swimming 265, 267–8
Swimming pool 71
Swiss Alps 239
"A Symphony of Lights" 64
Syrian Desert 168

T

T-Series 31
Tallgrass Prairie National Preserve 199
Tamarack 177
Tampa Bay 246
Tampa Bay Lightning 258
Tanzania 170
Tarantino, Quentin 36
Tarantulas 138
Taurasi, Diana 243
Team USA 243, 262
Teapot Dome Scandal 230
Teapot Dome Service Station 230
Techichi 151
Teeth 124
Telescopes 75, 84
Temperature 157, 176
Tennessee 225
Tennis 237, 254–5
Terra-cotta warriors 76–7
Tetris 98
Teutonic Knights 67
Texas 183, 226
Thailand 115
Thanksgiving 204
Theme parks 58–9
Thermal springs 233

Thompson, Tina 243
Thrust SSC 52
Thunder Over Louisville 200
Tibet 166
Tiger 119
Tightrope walking 239
TikTok 17, 24, 85, 92–3, 265
Timmerman Airport 232
Titanosaur 125
Toltec civilization 151
Tombs 76–7
Tomlin, Chris 188
Tomlinson, LaDainian 245
Toney, Tyler 241
Tony Awards 42
Tops Diner 215
Toronto Maple Leafs 256
Tortoise 150
The Tortured Poets
  Department (Taylor Swift) 9
Towers, Myke 13
Township 88
Toys 24, 237
Trailers 51
Trains 53
Transport 44–59
Trees 157, 158–9
Trenches 164
Trew, Arisa 266
TripAdvisor 73
Tsunami Surge 59
Turkey 146
Turkmenistan 169
Tusks 124
TV shows 26–8, 30
Tweets 87
Twin Towers 239
Tyrannosaurus rex 209
Tyus, Wyomia 193

U
Uganda 170
Umbrellas 179
United Arab Emirates 64
United States 14, 149, 156,
  172–3, 175, 177, 184–233, 252,
  277
University of Connecticut
  Huskies 243
University of Southern
  California 247
Uruguay 251
Urine 85
US Constitution 191
US Open 254, 255
USA International Ballet
  Competition 207
USC Trojans 247
USDA 217

Usher 28
Utah 227
Uttar Pradesh 178

V
Valeriana 62
Valley of Geysers 165
Vanderbilt, George 216
Vela, Carlos 249
Vermont 228
Versius 105
Verstappen, Max 260
Vettel, Sebastian 260
Viaducts 72
Videos 10, 89, 90–3
Vietnam 162–3
Virginia 229
Volleyball 236

W
Wade, Lestat 102
Walker, Maggie Lena 229
Wallen, Morgan 21
Wallis, Quvenzhané 34
Walls 74
Wampanoag people 204
Washington 230
Washington, George 203
Washington Olympics 197
Water coasters 59
Water lilies 161
Water parks 50, 59
Waves 171
Way, Danny 238
Weather 175–9, 183
Webber, Andrew Lloyd 40
Webster, Ian 157
West Virginia 231
Whale shark 126
Whales 124–5, 126
"What Was I Made For?" (Billie
  Eilish) 35
White, Shaun 275
White Mountains, California
  158
Whitehall 216
Whole Enchilada Fiesta 214
Wicked 25
Wight, Rev. Henry 222
Wildfires 172–3
Wildlife crossings 183
Williams 186
Williams, Ava 24
Williams, Serena 254
Williams, Suni 47
Williams, Venus 237, 254
Wilmore, Butch 47
Wilson, Lainey 18
Wimbledon 237, 254, 255

Winter Olympics 262, 272–5
Winter Paralympic Games 277
Winter X Games 238, 262
Wisconsin 232
Wittman Regional Airport 232
Wizz Air 84
WNBA 237, 242, 243
Wolferman's Bakery 220
Women 218, 229
Women's World Cup 252
World Championship Pumpkin
  Weigh-Off 160
World Dream 80
World Emoji Awards 104
World Health Organization
  (WHO) 142
World Meteorological
  Organization (WMO) 175, 176
World Series 248
World Surf League 261
World Trade Center 239
World Vert Championship 240
Worthington-Cox, Eleanor 43
Wyoming 233

X
X Games 238, 240, 275
X-43A plane 54

Y
Yangtze River 72, 170
Yankee, Daddy 10
Yas Marina Circuit 46
Yearbook photobooth 85
Yellow River 170
Yellowstone National Park 111,
  144, 165, 233
Yeoh, Michelle 33
YouTube 10, 30, 31, 89–91
Yup'ik 185

Z
Zambelli Fireworks 200
Zee Music Company 31
Zheng Haohao 265
Zillah 230
Ziolkowski, Korczak 224
Zoos 196
Zorn, Trischa 276

PHOTO CREDITS

Photos ©: cover top left: AP Photo/ Godofredo A. Vásquez; cover top right: Joseph Okpako/WireImage/ Getty Images; cover center: BFA/ Alamy Stock Photo; cover center left: TCD/Prod.DB/Alamy Stock Photo; cover center right: dpa picture alliance/Alamy Stock Photo; cover bottom center: TCD/Prod.DB/Alamy Stock Photo; cover bottom left: Barry King/Alamy Stock Photo; back cover top left: Patrick Pleul/picture alliance via Getty Images; back cover top right: Allstar Picture Library Limited/ Alamy Stock Photo; back cover bottom left: FlixPix/Alamy Stock Photo; back cover bottom right: Kevin Mazur/WireImage/Getty Images; 4–5, 19: Brooke Sutton/Getty Images; 6 top: AP Photo/Lindsey Wasson; 6 bottom: Daniel DeSlover/ZUMA Press Wire/Shutterstock; 7 top: Alex Slitz/ Getty Images; 7 center: Jeff Kravitz/ Getty Images for MTV; 7 bottom: ZUMA Press, Inc./Alamy Stock Photo; 8: Kevin Mazur/Getty Images for Live Nation; 9: Neilson Barnard/Getty Images for The Recording Academy; 10: GDA via AP Images; 11: Gareth Cattermole/Getty Images; 12: Prince Williams/Wireimage/Getty Images; 13: Scott Strazzante/San Francisco Chronicle via AP; 14: Marc Tielemans/ Alamy Stock Photo; 15: Aflo Co. Ltd./ Alamy Stock Photo; 16: Sthanlee Mirador/SipaUSA via AP Images; 17: John Shearer/Getty Images for The Recording Academy; 18: AFF-USA/ Shutterstock; 20: Victor Chavez/Getty Images for Spotify; 21: John Shearer/ Getty Images for MTV; 22–23, 25 bottom: Rob Latour/Shutterstock; 24 top: Indian Paintbrush/Kobal/ Shutterstock; 24 bottom: Heritage Auctions/HA.com; 25 top: Capital Pictures/Alamy Stock Photo; 25 center: TCD/Prod.DB/Alamy Stock Photo; 26: Cinematic/Alamy Stock Photo; 27: Album/Alamy Stock Photo; 28: UPI/Alamy Stock Photo; 29: TCD/ Prod.DB/Alamy Stock Photo; 30: Islandstock/Alamy Stock Photo; 31: Prodip Guha/Getty Images; 32: Photo 12/Alamy Stock Photo; 33: Anthony Harvey/Shutterstock; 34: Jim Smeal/ BEI/Shutterstock; 35: Evan Agostini/ Invision/AP; 36: Kevin Mazur/Getty Images; 37: Action Press/ Shutterstock; 38: TCD/Prod.DB/Alamy Stock Photo; 39: Collection Christophel/Alamy Stock Photo; 40: Peter Kramer/Getty Images; 41: ROSLAN RAHMAN/AFP via Getty Images; 42: Bruce Glikas/FilmMagic/ Getty Images; 43: Richard Young/ Shutterstock; 44–45, 50: Joe Raedle/ Getty Images; 46 top: Waleed Zein/ Anadolu via Getty Images; 46 bottom: Exotica.im/Universal Images Group via Getty Images; 47 top: SpaceX/ UPI/Shutterstock; 47 center: NASA; 47 bottom: NTSB/UPI/Shutterstock; 48: Jeffrey Greenberg/UIG via Getty Images; 49: Rolls-Royce Motor Cars; 51 bottom: Jonathan Hordle/REX/ Shutterstock; 52: David Madison/ Getty Images; 54: NASA; 55: NASA Johns Hopkins APL; 56 top: NASA; 56 bottom: NASA; 57: NASA; 58: imageBROKER.com GmbH & Co. KG/Alamy Stock Photo; 59: Hurricane Harbor Chicago; 62 top: Riccardo Milani/Hans Lucas/AFP via Getty Images; 62 center: Kyle Stevens/ Shutterstock; 62 bottom: Luke Auld-Thomas, Marcello A. Canuto, Adriana Velázquez Morlet, Francisco Estrada- Belli, David Chatelain, Diego Matadamas, Michelle Pigott, Juan Carlos Fernández, 2024; 63 bottom: AP Photo/Mark Schiefelbein; 64: Michael Ho Wai Lee/SOPA Images/ LightRocket via Getty Images; 65: Eric Lafforgue/Art In All Of Us/Corbis via Getty Images; 67: Jim Zuckerman/ Alamy Stock Photo; 70: Mike Greenslade/VWPics via AP Images; 71: Crystal Lagoons/REX/ Shutterstock; 72: Su Yang/Costfoto/ Future Publishing via Getty Images; 74: Living facades by ANS Global; 75: NASA/ESA/CSA/STScI; 76–77: JUN LI/Alamy Stock Photo; 78 bottom: Courtesy of Neeraj Daga; 79: Ritzau Scanpix/Sipa USA via AP Images; 80: Edward Wong/South China Morning Post via Getty Images; 82–83 , 85 bottom: RICHARD A. BROOKS/AFP via Getty Images; 84 top: NASA/ESA/ CSA/STScI; 84 bottom: AP Photo/ Armando Franca; 85 top: Moviestore Collection Ltd/Alamy Stock Photo; 86: Yasser Bakhsh/Getty Images; 87 logos: Ejevica/Dreamstime.com; 87: Aflo/Shutterstock; 88: Courtesy of Hungry Studio; 89: Stephen Chung/ Alamy Stock Photo; 90: JOSE COELHO/EPA-EFE/Shutterstock; 91: Ryan's World; 92: gotpap/ Bauer-Griffin/GC Images/Getty Images; 93: Jay L Clendenin/Los Angeles Times/Shutterstock; 94: Lionel Hahn/Abaca/Sipa via AP Images; 95: Amanda Edwards/ WireImage/Getty Images; 98: maximimages.com/Alamy Stock Photo; 99: AP Photo/John Raoux; 100: Asiaselects/Alamy Stock Photo; 101: Stephen Lam/Getty Images; 102–103: theodore liasi/Alamy Stock Photo; 105: CMR Surgical; 106–107: CTK/Alamy Stock Photo; 110 top: Lev Radin/Shutterstock; 110 bottom: Justin Sullivan/Getty Images; 111 top: Laumer, I.B., Rahman, A., Rahmaeti, T. et al.; 111 center: Erin Braaten; 111 bottom: Sea Life Melbourne Aquarium; 113: Kim Taylor/NPL/ Minden Pictures; 115: Steve Downeranth/Pantheon/SuperStock; 123: Images & Stories/Alamy Stock Photo; 124: Bryan & Cherry Alexander/Science Source; 125: WaterFrame/Alamy Stock Photo; 127: F1online digitale Bildagentur GmbH/ Alamy Stock Photo; 128: Ksumano/ Dreamstime.com; 131: dpa picture alliance archive/Alamy Stock Photo; 133: Tim Laman/Minden Pictures; 134: Chris Knightstan/Pantheon/

MATH GENIUS BABY DEV

In May 2024, "Baby Dev" became the youngest-ever contestant to appear on *America's Got Talent*. In the show, he wowed the judges with his incredible math skills. Devan, from Commack in Long Island, New York, was two years old at the time, but it seems his interest goes back to when he was just four months old—he would get upset if his parents switched an early-learning channel from math to something else. On the TV show, Baby Dev deftly dealt with 7 x 9 (63) and 44 + 13 (57), drawing gasps from the crowd. But it was when he multiplied 79 x 7 that the judges showed true amazement. It did not take Baby Dev very long to arrive at the answer (553), and as one member of the audience noted, he did not even use his fingers for counting!